KT-173-028

Terry Harrison's
WATERCOLOUR
SECRETS

A lifetime of painting techniques

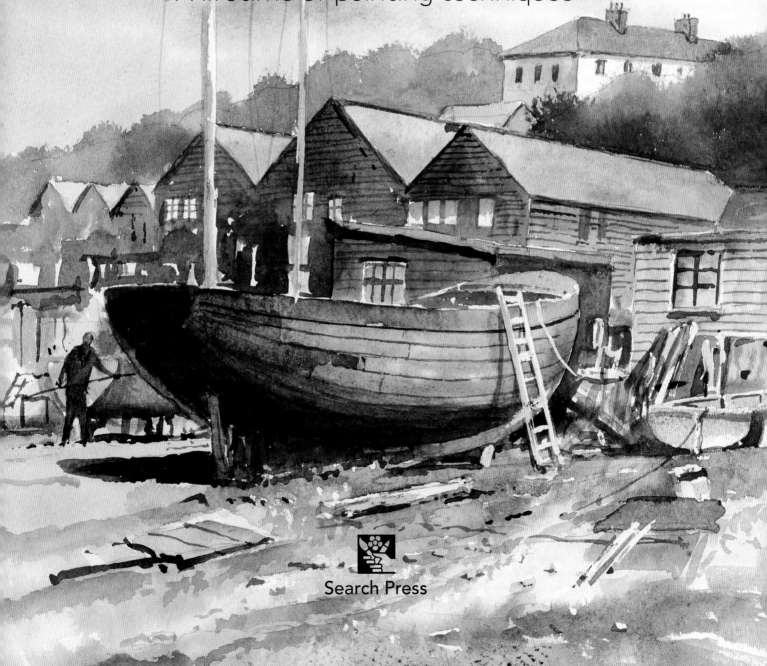

Search Press

Contents

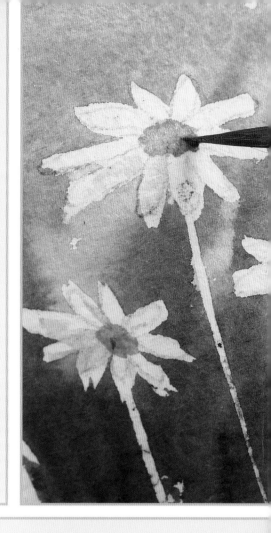

About the author   6

Introduction   8

What to buy   10

    PAPER   10

    BRUSHES   13

    PAINTS   19

    OTHER USEFUL ITEMS   20

Using photographs   22

Colour   28

    MIXING WATERCOLOURS   34

Techniques   38

    WASHES   38

    WET INTO WET   40

    WET ON DRY   43

    DRY BRUSHWORK   44

    GLAZING   46

    MASKING   48

    LIFTING OUT   54

Special effects   58

Troubleshooting   62

Skies   66

Distance   72

Fields   74

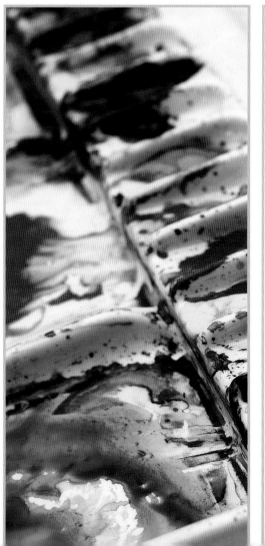

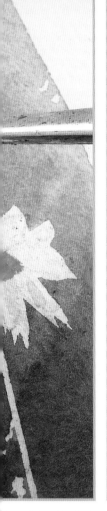

Trees	76
Grasses	84
Flowers	86
Mountains	92
Water	94
Beaches	102
Rocks	104
Cliffs	106
Boats	108

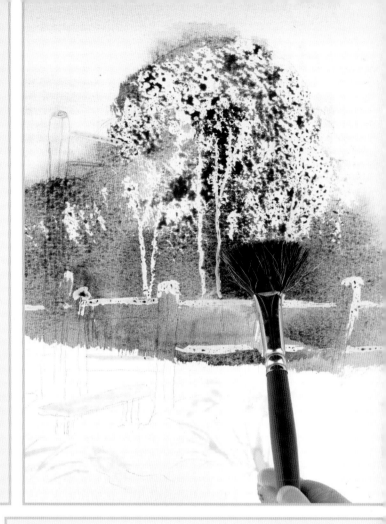

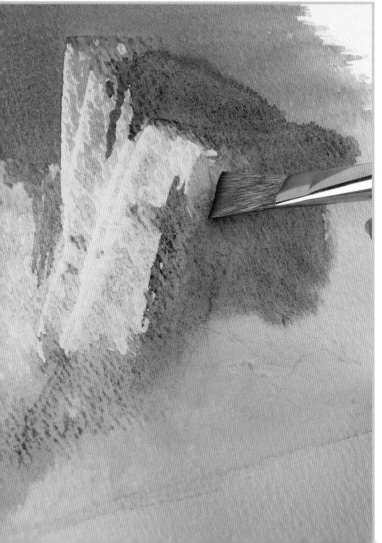

Roofs		110
Walls		112
Windows & doors		116
	WINDOWS	116
	DOORS	117
Stiles, gates & fences		120
Winter scenes		122
Figures & animals		126
Index		128

Pearse Street Branch
Brainse Sráid Piarsach
Tel: 6744888

About the author

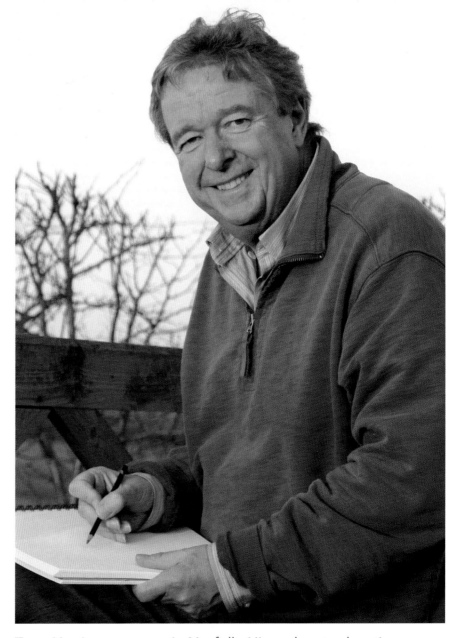

Terry Harrison grew up in Norfolk. His early art education was basic and he never dreamed that he would become an artist. At fifteen, Terry moved to Hampshire and was inspired by a brilliant art teacher. He took O- and A-levels in art, then won a place at Farnham Art School at the age of sixteen. He became a graphic artist, but continued to paint in his spare time. In 1984 Terry gave up his job to paint full-time. He demonstrates to artists' groups and teaches on painting holidays. He has also developed a range of his own brushes and paints. He is the author of many best-selling books on painting with acrylics and watercolours. Terry now lives in the Cotswolds.

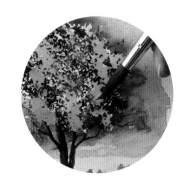
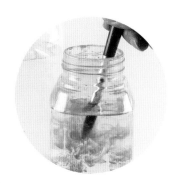
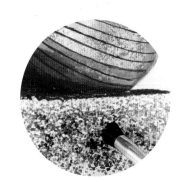

Terry Harrison's
WATERCOLOUR
SECRETS

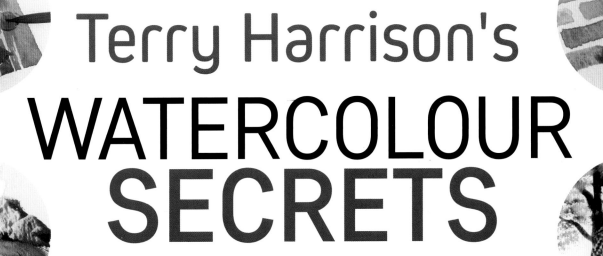
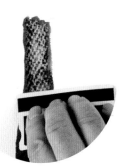
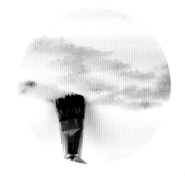
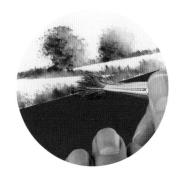

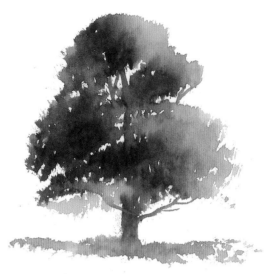

Acknowledgements

Special thanks to my wife, Fiona Peart, for all
her support and help with this book. Also
my thanks go to my long-suffering editor,
Sophie Kersey.

First published in 2017

Search Press Limited
Wellwood, North Farm Road,
Tunbridge Wells, Kent TN2 3DR

Includes material from the following books published by
Search Press: *Terry's Top Tips for Watercolour Artists*, 2008;
30 Minute Artist: Painting Water in Watercolour, 2013 and
Rustic Buildings & Barns in Watercolour, 2009

Text copyright © Terry Harrison 2017

Photographs by Roddy Paine Photographic Studios
and by Paul Bricknell at Search Press Studio

Photographs and design copyright ©
Search Press Ltd, 2017

All rights reserved. No part of this book, text, photographs
or illustrations may be reproduced or transmitted in any form
or by any means by print, photoprint, microfilm, microfiche,
photocopier, internet or in any way known or as yet unknown,
or stored in a retrieval system, without written permission
obtained beforehand from Search Press.

ISBN: 978-1-78221-329-1

The Publishers and author can accept no responsibility for
any consequences arising from the information, advice or
instructions given in this publication.

Suppliers
If you have difficulty in obtaining any of the materials
and equipment mentioned in this book, please contact
Terry Harrison at:

Telephone: +44 (0) 1451 820014

Website: www.terryharrison.com

Alternatively, visit the Search Press website:
www.searchpress.com

Publishers' note
All the step-by-step photographs in this book feature the
author, Terry Harrison, demonstrating how to paint with
watercolours. No models have been used.

Printed in China

Bluebell wood

This woodland glade has more than a touch of spring about it: there are plenty of spring colours in the foliage and a gorgeous carpet of bluebells. Most of the tree trunks were masked first with masking fluid, not just the silver birches.

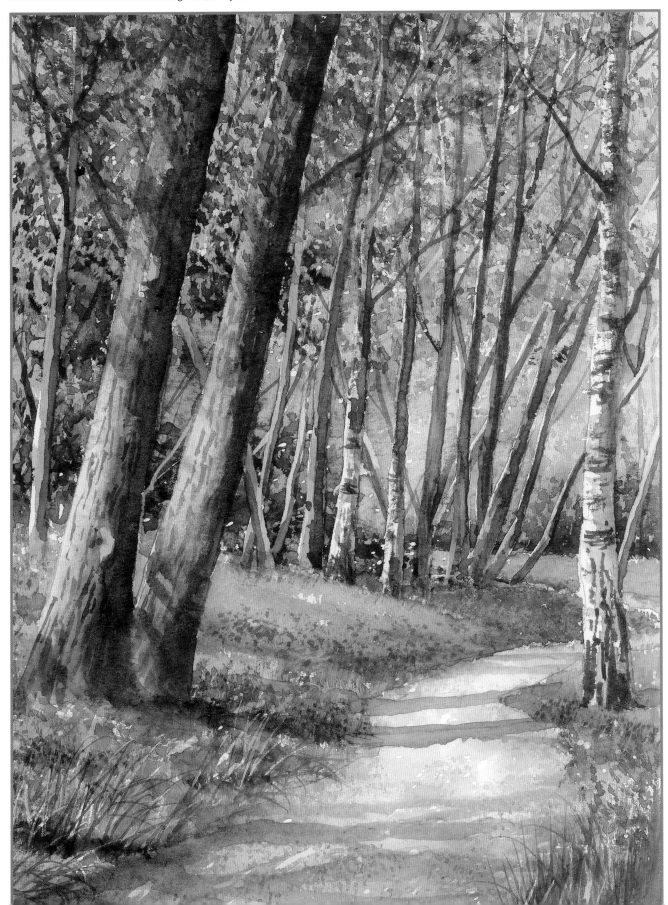

Introduction

My aim in teaching art has always been to make painting more accessible by helping to make the techniques easier. I have even created my own range of brushes, specially designed to make it easier for the beginner to achieve a variety of effects.

Much of my advice on watercolour techniques is based on common sense: for instance, to achieve wet into wet effects, the paper surface has to be wet, not merely damp or beginning to dry! Years of experience of painting and teaching have meant that I have accumulated a wealth of handy tips for successful painting, and in this book I pass on my secrets, from the ones I first learned to completely new ones.

I have been painting and drawing since I can remember. I used to copy the characters in my weekly comics, and the first watercolour that I can remember doing was a painting of a budgerigar from the front of a packet of Trill birdseed. You can see that I learned from an early age that the use of reference material is very important! Now, with the help of the internet, an artist can source almost any subject or image at the click of a mouse. Before this was an option, I managed to amass a collection of photographs taken on holidays or while travelling, then carefully filed away for future reference. Using your own photographs means you do not have to worry about copyright laws, which few people seem to understand.

In this book I will share with you many secrets, dispel some myths and hopefully take the mystery out of watercolour painting.

Opposite

Rocky shoreline
There is plenty of action on the shoreline in this painting, capturing the moment when a wave crashes into the rocks and beach. All you need is some kitchen paper and masking fluid, a plastic card for the rocks and a spattering of paint for the beach. All the techniques can be found within the pages of this book.

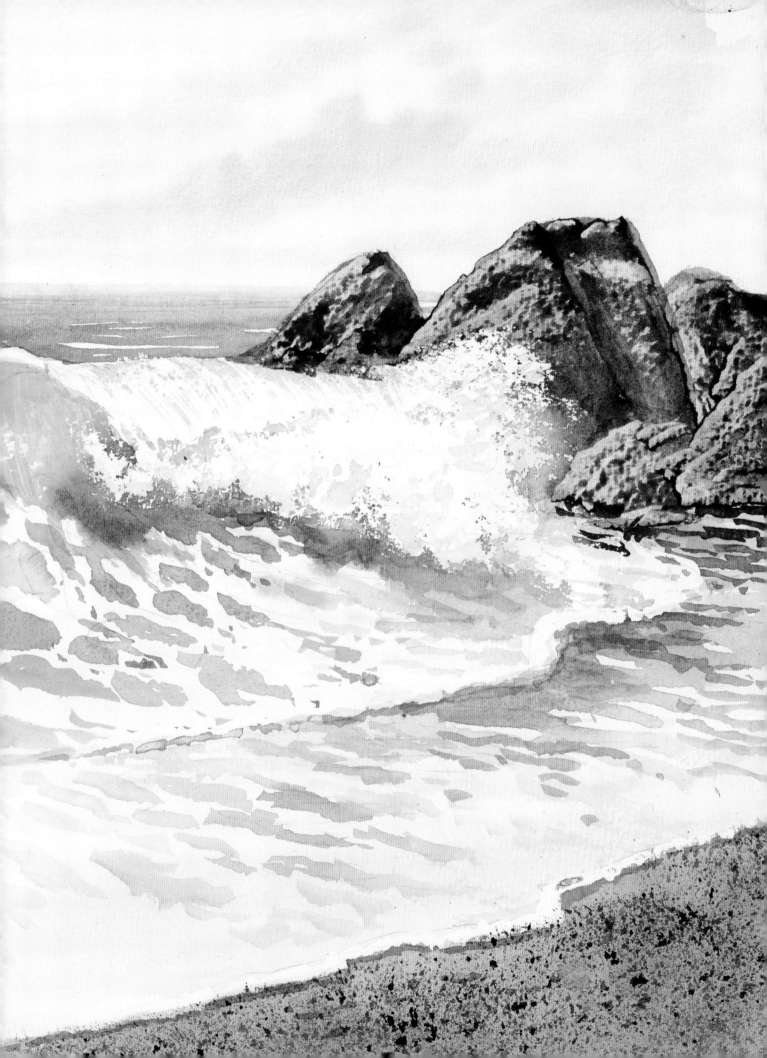

What to buy

Paper

Whatever paper you start painting on will probably be the paper you stay with. The reason for this is that you learn how to paint on a certain surface, and if you change to another surface, you need to adapt your style. For instance, if you paint a wash, it will work perfectly on one surface but will not be right on another. All the paper used in this book is Bockingford, a wood pulp paper which is not too absorbent and is a good surface for masking fluid. It is white as opposed to cream and it is an inexpensive, good quality watercolour paper.

You can also buy tinted papers in colours such as grey, pale blue, cream and oatmeal. By choosing a coloured background to your painting, you can enhance the mood.

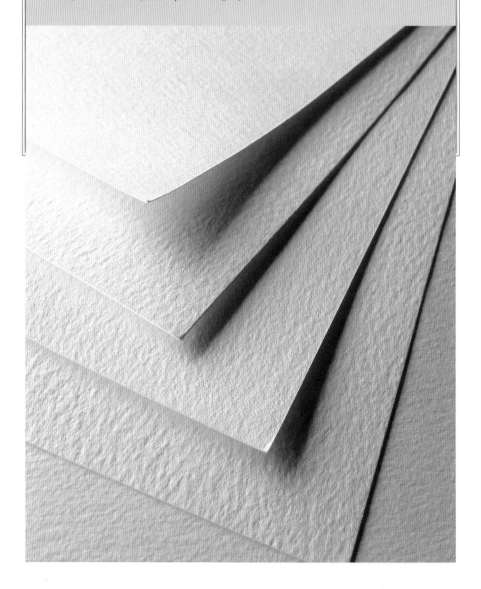

1 **CHOOSING THE RIGHT PAPER**

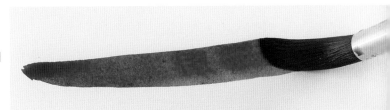

Watercolour paper comes in three surfaces, Hot Pressed (smooth), Not (called this because it is not hot pressed; it is in fact cold pressed) and Rough. The hot pressed paper shown on the right is suitable for botanical and detailed paintings, portraiture and fine detail.

Rough paper is an ideal surface for landscapes and seascapes, as the surface helps give the impression of texture and is particularly useful for the dry brush technique.

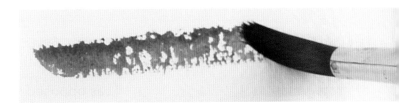

2 **PREVENTING COCKLING**

Cockling occurs when you apply a wash to the paper surface. The fibres in the paper soak up the water and expand. If the paper is unevenly wetted, the fibres expand at different rates and cockling occurs. This is why artists are recommended to stretch paper by soaking it, taping it to a drawing board and allowing it to dry. The paper shrinks as it dries, but because it is taped at the edges, it dries fully stretched. I find, however, that although the paper dries almost flat, some cockling will still occur when you apply washes. I also find that stretching paper affects the paper, as some of the size is removed. For these reasons I don't bother to stretch paper.

The simplest way to flatten a painting that has cockled is to turn it face down, wet the back of it (don't over-wet it), allow the water to soak in, and when the paper is fully expanded, put a drawing board over it and weigh it down with a pile of books. Let the painting dry overnight and it will dry completely flat.

Another solution to cockling is to use a heavy paper. I use a 300gsm (140lb) paper, but to avoid cockling altogether, use an even heavier paper.

Finally, you could use the method shown on page 65 to prevent cockling.

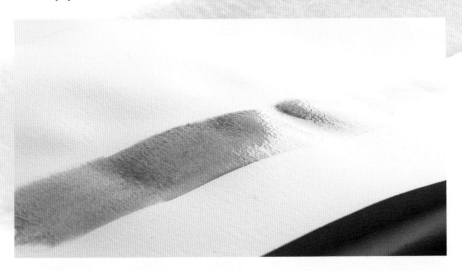

Leabharlanna Poiblí Chathair Bhaile Átha Cliath
Dublin City Public Libraries

3 USING TINTED PAPER

Tinted watercolour paper has been around for years, but few art supply stores stock it, which is a shame. The one I use is Bockingford, which comes in four different shades: grey, blue, cream and oatmeal. Simply by changing the colour of the paper, you can alter or enhance the mood of a painting. Choose blue or grey for a winter scene, or a warm tint such as cream or oatmeal for a sunset. Here I have painted the same scene on two contrasting papers and created two entirely different paintings.

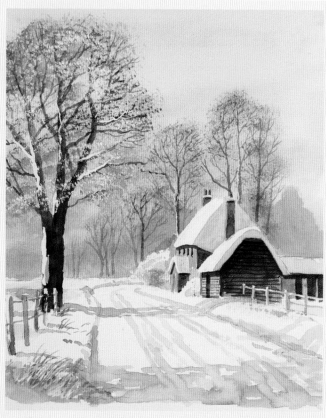

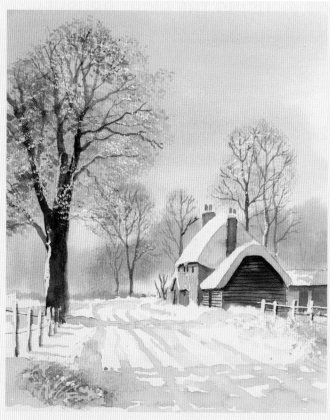

The blue tinted paper has enhanced the cool feeling of the end of the day; it has a real chill factor.

Using oatmeal-tinted Bockingford might seem a strange choice of paper for a snow scene but the paper enhances the warm glow in the sky while the cool blues used to paint the shadows tell you it's a snowy day in winter.

Brushes

Many artists adapt standard watercolour brushes to suit their needs. I have gone one step further and created my own range of brushes, designed to help you achieve the best effects with the minimum effort. You can of course choose brushes from other ranges; look for the attributes described below.

4 USING THE RIGHT BRUSHES

Shown on the right are the brushes you will need to create the effects shown in this book. The brushes also come in 'px' versions, which have a clear acrylic resin handle with the end shaped specially for scraping out techniques.

The **half-rigger** has long hair with a very fine point. It holds quite a lot of paint and is ideal for adding very fine details wet on dry. It is good for painting grasses and flower stalks.

The **small detail brush** is the smallest of the round brushes in my range. It is good for painting fine details.

The **medium detail brush** is the workhorse of the range, the one you reach for most often. It holds quite a lot of paint but still goes to a fine point, and is good for painting any but the finest details.

The **large detail brush** holds a lot of paint; it is ideal for washes, yet it goes to quite a fine point, making it a very versatile brush.

The **fan stippler** is good for painting trees with a stippling technique. The blend of natural hair and bristle creates a range of textural effects that can be used to mimic elements of nature such as leaves.

The **19mm (¾in) flat brush** is useful for washes and for painting water. It can be used with a side-to-side motion to create horizontal lines such as ripples on water.

The **foliage brush** is excellent for producing leafy effects and it can also be used for texture on buildings, footpaths and walls.

The **wizard** is made from a blend of natural hair, twenty per cent of which is slightly longer than the rest and forms small points. It is good for grasses and reflections.

The **golden leaf brush** holds lots of paint, so is ideal for sky washes or for water. It is good for stippling trees and foliage and for painting texture.

The **fan gogh** is thicker than most fan brushes and holds plenty of paint. It is good for trees, grasses and reflections in water.

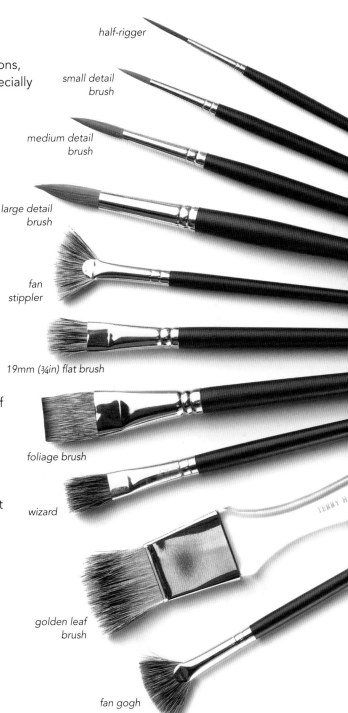

half-rigger

small detail brush

medium detail brush

large detail brush

fan stippler

19mm (¾in) flat brush

foliage brush

wizard

golden leaf brush

fan gogh

5 USING THE FUNKY POUNCER: STIPPLING FOLIAGE

The funky pouncer is made from strips of durable leather bound together with a nickel ferrule. It has a clear acrylic resin handle and a soft, non-slip rubber grip. It is designed to create texture by stippling (pouncing).

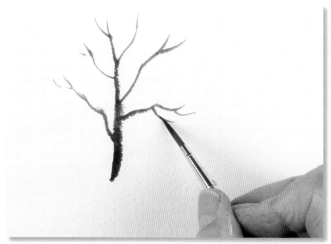

1 Paint the trunk and branches with the small detail brush and burnt umber.

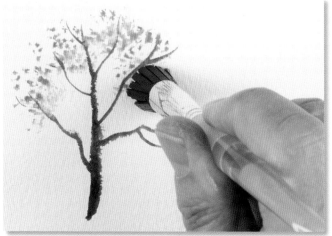

2 Dip the funky pouncer in sunlit green and use it to stipple foliage.

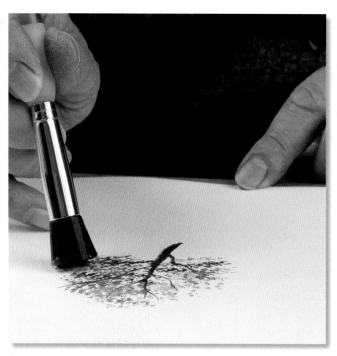

3 Add country green to the mix and stipple this on to paint the shadowed parts of the tree.

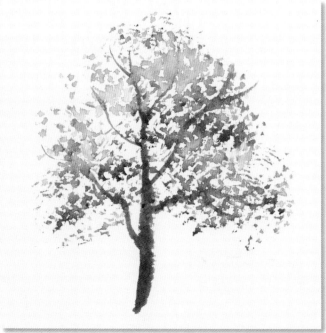

The finished tree.

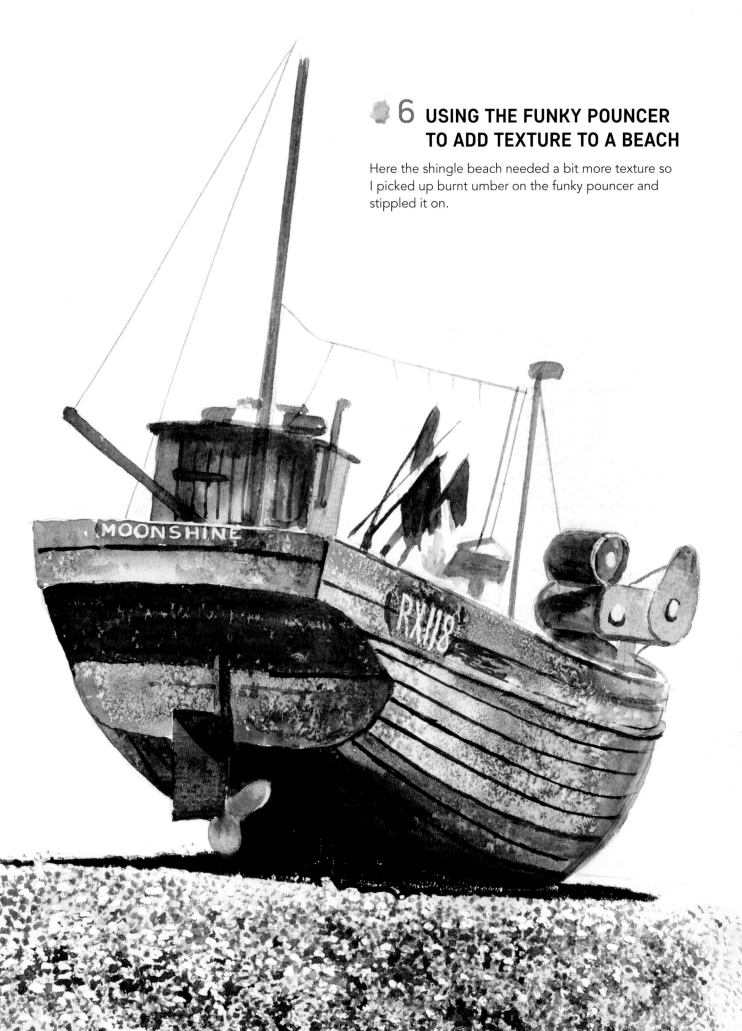

6 USING THE FUNKY POUNCER TO ADD TEXTURE TO A BEACH

Here the shingle beach needed a bit more texture so I picked up burnt umber on the funky pouncer and stippled it on.

✎7 USING THE DEERFOOT STIPPLER

This brush is a mixture of bristle and hair, round in shape with the end cut away at an angle. It is ideal for stippling foliage and creating textures.

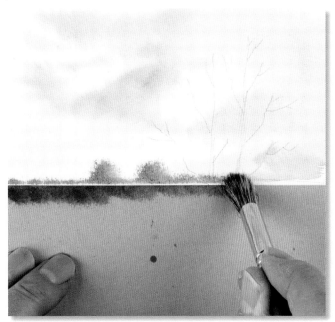

1 Paint the sky and allow it to dry. Use a paper mask to get a straight horizon and use the deerfoot stippler to stipple a blue-green mix of ultramarine and midnight green along the edge, creating distant trees.

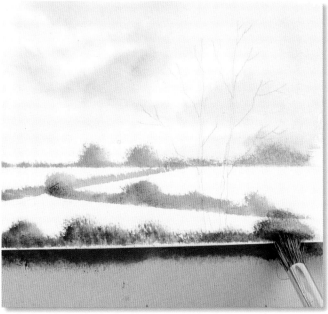

2 Angle the paper mask and stipple hedges coming forwards with country olive. Vary the height to include larger bushes and trees. Continue moving the paper mask and changing the angle towards the foreground.

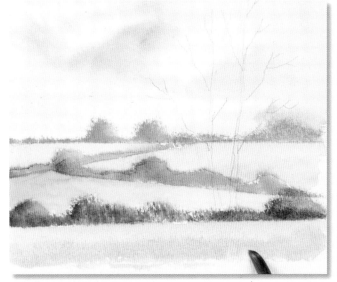

3 Use the medium detail brush to paint a weak mix of sunlit green in the distant fields, adding raw sienna as you come forwards. Paint a bright mix of sunlit green and raw sienna in the foreground. Allow to dry.

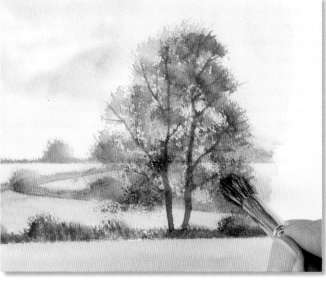

4 Paint the trunks and branches of the foreground trees with the half-rigger and a mix of burnt umber and country olive. Use the deerfoot stippler to stipple sunlit green on the lit parts of the tree, then stipple the shadowed areas with country olive.

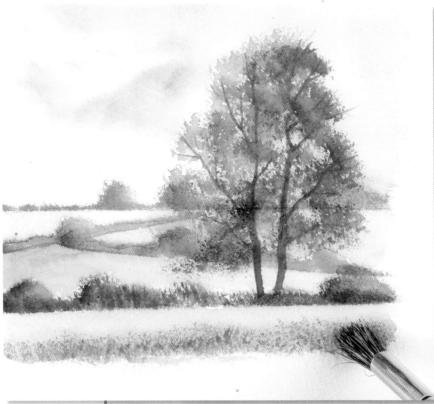

5 Flick up grasses with country olive in the foreground, still using the deerfoot stippler.

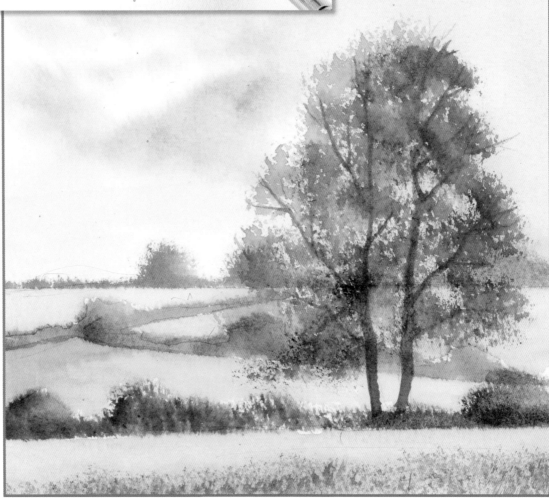

The finished painting.

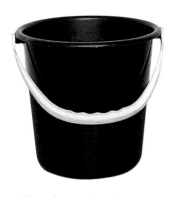

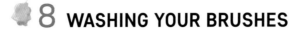

8 WASHING YOUR BRUSHES

In my studio I use a bucket to wash out my brushes. This is because the more water you use, the cleaner your brushes become. There is little point in trying to clean your brushes in a small jam jar. Also, the water stays cleaner for longer.

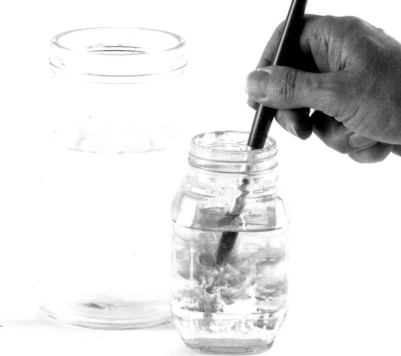

The alternative is to use two water pots, one for washing your brushes and the second for mixing your colours with clean water.

When painting on location, I carry my paints in an ice cream tub. I tip the paints out on arrival and fill the ice cream tub with water. I use water from a nearby river, stream, water fountain or café.

Never leave brushes standing in water, as this will bend the tip of the brush, and the water will soak up into the wooden handle. The wood then expands and the paint on the handle cracks and peels off.

9 STORING YOUR BRUSHES

I carry my brushes in a folding brush case with a zip. You open the case and all your brushes are in front of you, ready to use. What could be simpler?

A brush roll can crush brushes such as fan brushes and flats. I certainly would not recommend storing brushes in a tube. If you store wet brushes in a tube and it is held upside down, the bristles will bend, and when dry, they can remain bent.

At the end of a painting session, run the brushes under a tap, pat them dry with kitchen paper, reshape them if necessary and return them to your brush case ready to paint your next masterpiece.

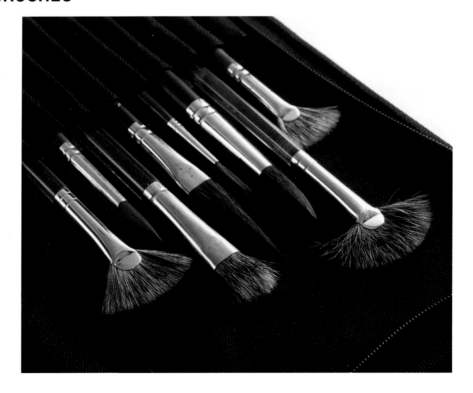

Paints

Watercolour paints come either in pans or in tubes. As with paper, people tend to stick with whatever they started with. Generally, tube colours are suitable for studio work, as you are likely to paint on a larger scale, and will use bigger brushes which do not fit into pans. When you are painting outside, you might find a compact set of pans more convenient and easier to carry. You can buy either student quality or artist quality watercolour paints. I would recommend that you start with artist quality as they have a higher pigment content, in other words there is more colour and less filling.

10 CHOOSING THE RIGHT PAINT

If you are painting large washes, it is best to use tube colours in artist quality. If you use student colours, you use a lot of paint to achieve the same colour, so the money you save on buying the cheaper paint turns out to be a false economy.

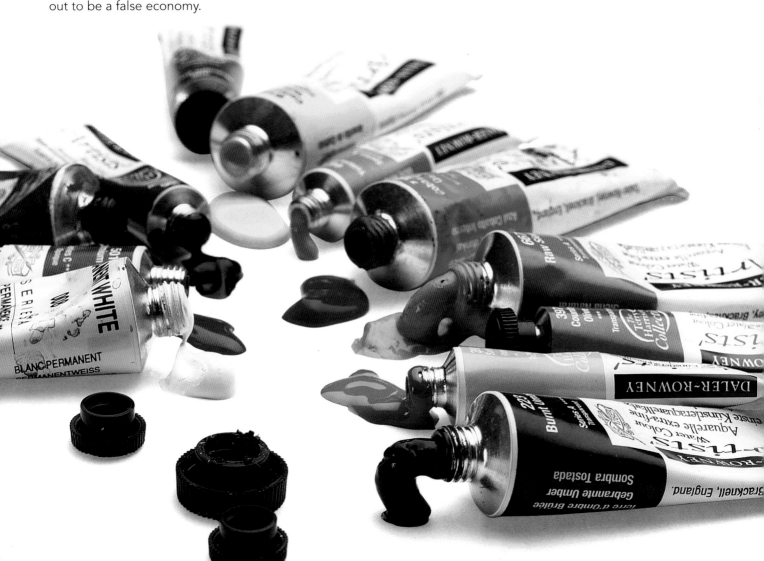

Other useful items

Watercolour painting is not just about paints and brushes – you might need other items to help you achieve that finished painting. Here is a selection of extra items you should not be without.

 ### 11 RULING PEN

Sometimes called a bow pen or a drawing office pen, this is used for applying masking fluid, as the fluid does not stick to the metal. It is ideal for masking out grasses or, with the aid of a straight edge, long straight lines. You can also use it to apply paint or ink to a painting.

 ### 12 ERASER

Ideal for enhancing your drawing rather than correcting mistakes! Before painting, it is always a good idea to remove excess pencil marks. I use a hard eraser rather than a putty eraser, because a putty eraser tends to smudge the pencil line rather than removing it.

 ### 13 KITCHEN PAPER

This is ideal for removing excess water from your paint brushes. You can use it for lifting out colour from a painting. It can be used to mop up puddles of watercolour on a painting, helping to prevent 'cauliflowers'. It is also useful for cleaning out your palette.

 ### 14 SOAP

This is applied to a brush before using masking fluid. This forms a barrier between the hairs of the brush and the masking fluid and makes cleaning the brush much easier.

 ### 15 PENCIL

I use a 2B pencil for drawing as it gives you the option of achieving dark or light tones and is easy to erase.

 ### 16 MASKING TAPE

This is used to tape your watercolour paper to a drawing board. Tape the painting at the top, not all the way round, so that when you apply water to the paper, it has room to expand. You can then tape it at the bottom while it is wet.

 ### 17 MASKING FLUID

This is a liquid latex which, when applied to paper, dries quickly and creates a resist. You can then paint over it, and when the paint is dry, you can remove the masking fluid by rubbing it with your fingers, to reveal white paper underneath.

 ### 18 PLASTIC CARD

This can be used to great effect for creating texture on tree trunks, rocks, cliffs and mountains.

 ### 19 PENCIL SHARPENER

Always keep your pencil sharp!

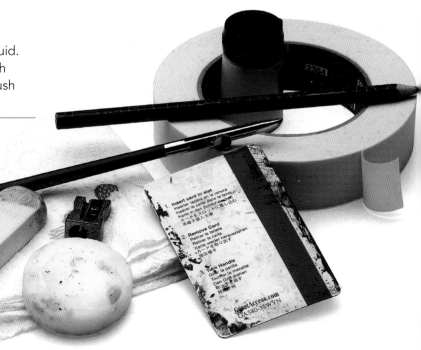

🪶20 SPONGE

A sponge can be used to apply masking fluid for some interesting textured effects. It is also used damp to lift out colour.

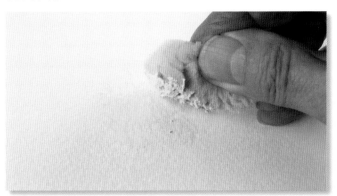

🪶23 COLOUR SHAPER

This can be used to apply masking fluid. Some have a larger and a smaller end so you can vary the effects you create.

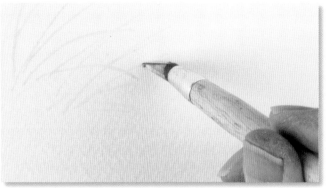

🪶21 MATERIALS FOR SPECIAL EFFECTS

Salt, candle wax, acrylic texture paste, watercolour ground and cling film can all be used to create special effects.

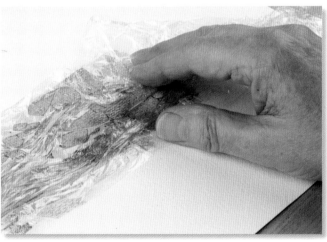

🪶24 MAGIC WATERCOLOUR ERASER

This is a block of plastic foam impregnated with a cleaning product, usually sold for cleaning. It removes dried watercolour as if by magic, and can be used for lifting out or erasing mistakes.

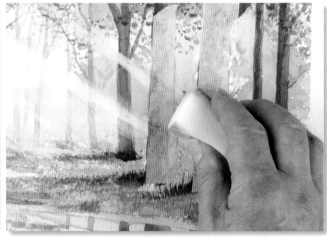

🪶22 HAIRDRYER

This is used to speed up drying times to stop you from overpainting on a wet surface.

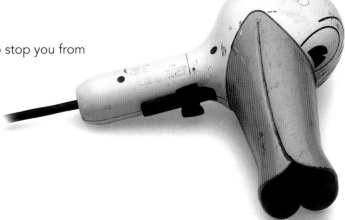

Using photographs

There is nothing wrong with using photographs as reference for a painting. Most artists use photographic reference as an aid. The key to it is not to copy the images exactly. It is very difficult to achieve the perfection of the photograph, but using it as a starting point, you can alter the view to achieve an almost perfect painting.

Make sure you take lots of photographs from different angles. Using a computer, you can enlarge an image to the size you want and trace it straight onto watercolour paper. If you do not have a computer, you can enlarge the image on a photocopier.

➤ *Moonshine*

I found this picture In my file of boats. It is a fishing boat moored high and dry on the shingle beach. For the painting, I removed the boat on the left and simplified the background to a silhouette of the boatyard sheds.

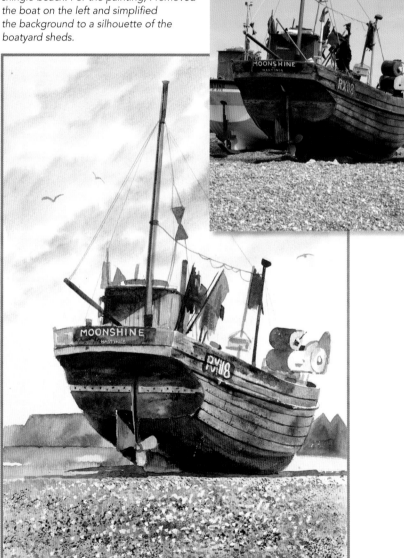

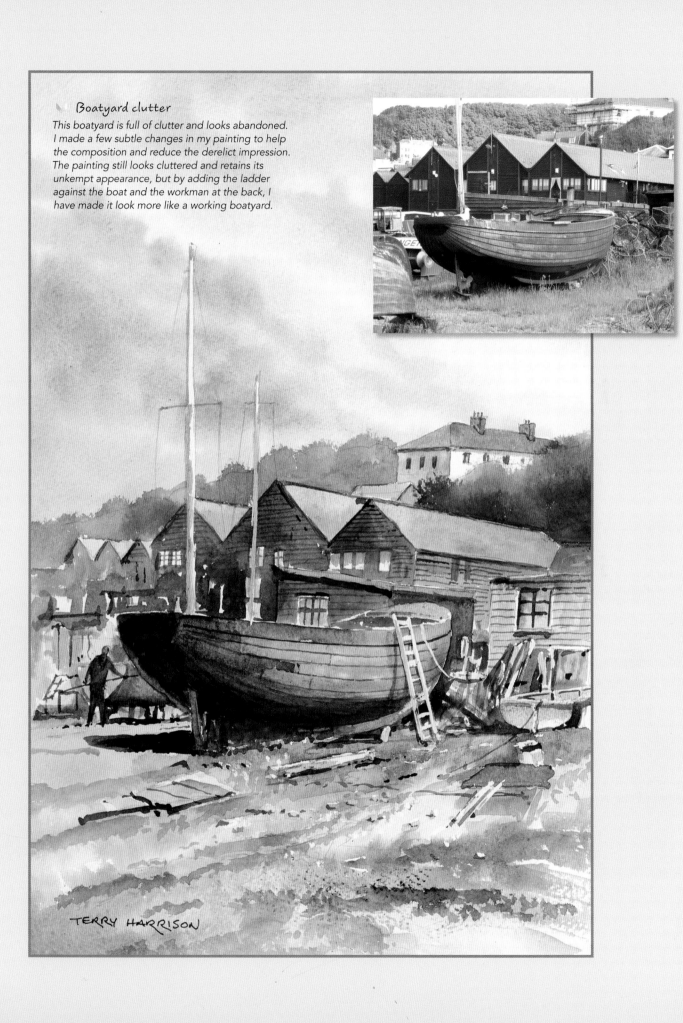

Boatyard clutter

This boatyard is full of clutter and looks abandoned.
I made a few subtle changes in my painting to help
the composition and reduce the derelict impression.
The painting still looks cluttered and retains its
unkempt appearance, but by adding the ladder
against the boat and the workman at the back, I
have made it look more like a working boatyard.

TERRY HARRISON

25 COLLECTING REFERENCE MATERIAL

Over the years I have collected a wealth of reference material which I use for my painting. I take a lot of photographs of the same subject but from different angles. This might be a view or just a shot of something interesting that I could add to a future painting. Download your photographs and file them away into reference folders in categories such as boats, skies, rivers and streams, bluebell woods and stiles – whatever you want to paint. This will save you time when you are looking for a certain image.

The biggest change in reference collecting is the internet. It is now possible to use search engines to find an image in almost any category you can think of. The only problem with using images from the internet is the risk of copyright infringement. If the image is just used as a reference or guide, or simply as inspiration, then there is no problem, but remember it is always best to use your own photographs where possible.

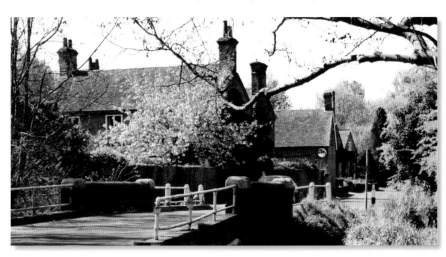

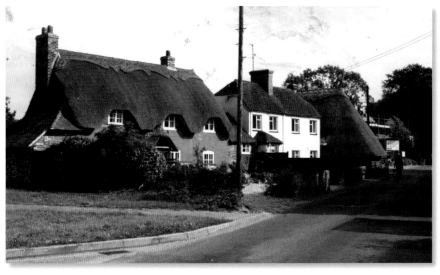

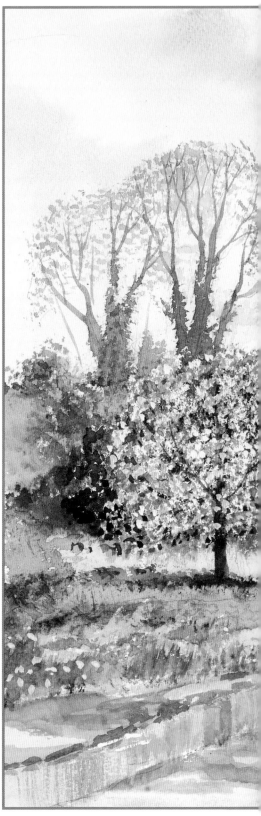

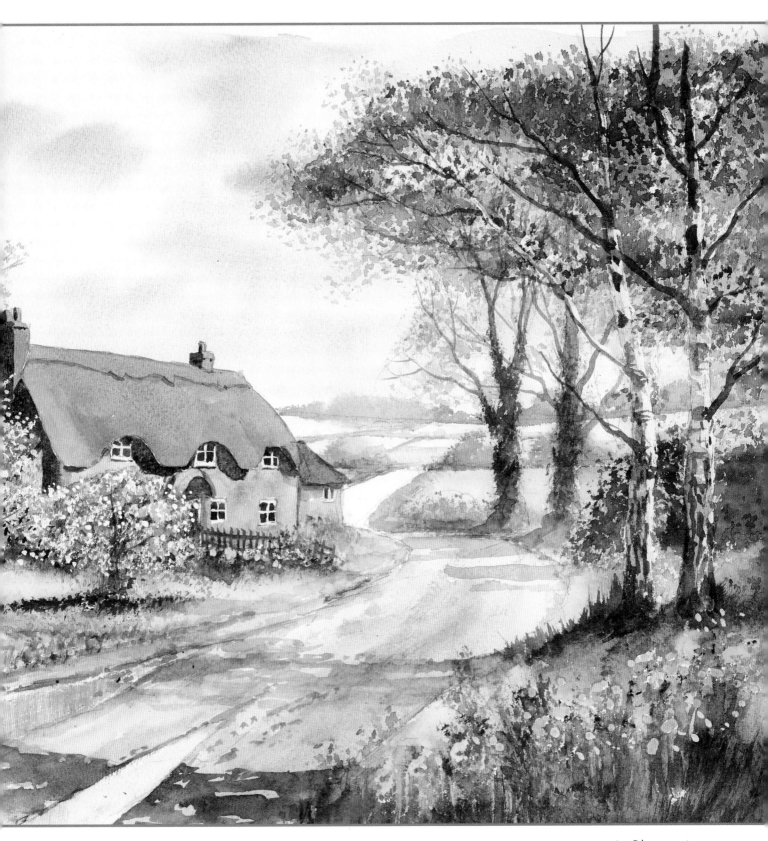

▲ Blossom time

Starting with the photograph of the cottage as my focal point, I used the blossom trees from my tree file as well as other trees to frame the cottage. The road leads you past the cottage and off into the distance.

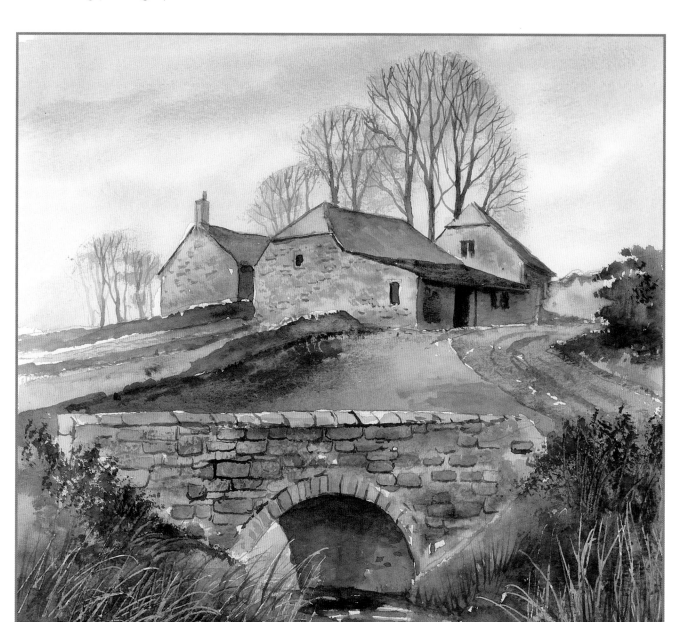

🖌 Country bridge

The painting above was composed from the two photographs shown opposite, selected from around twenty shots of the same scene. As you can see, I have used one photograph as a reference for the bridge, and the other as a reference for the buildings. Combining the two elements, you can create a painting of the scene which is not factually accurate but makes for a more pleasing composition.

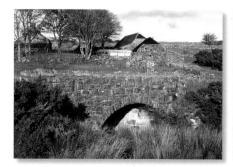

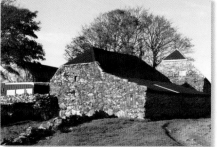

Hard day's work

This painting is a composite of two photographs. I wanted the tractor to be the focal point and the sunlit barn to be the backdrop. When photographing the scene, I waited for the tractor to come round to face in the right direction, zoomed in with the camera to capture the close-up details, then repositioned the tractor in the foreground.

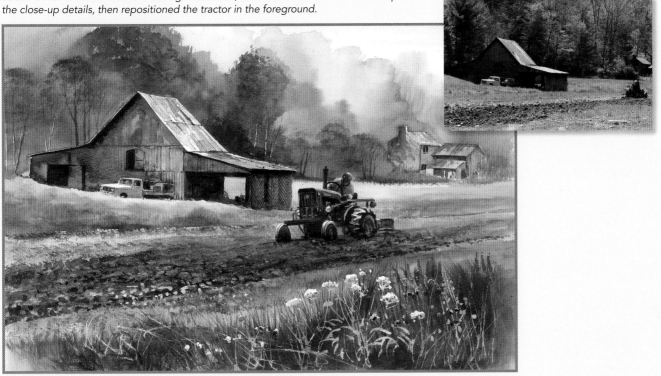

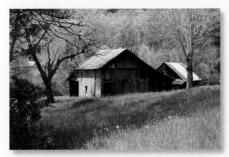

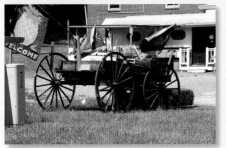

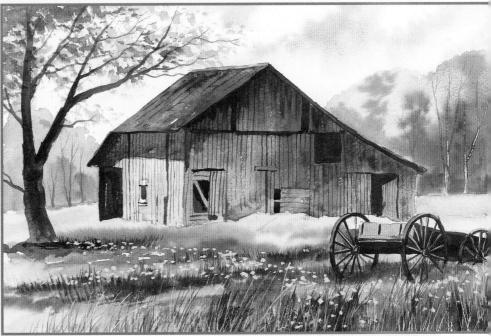

High country barn

For this painting, I used two photographs for my reference. The barn as a subject was fine, but the composition was a little flat. I therefore looked for something to fill the foreground and add some interest that would lead the viewer into the painting. I found an old wagon in my file called 'carts and wagons', which filled the gap perfectly.

Colour

I often hear artists sing the praises of using only a limited selection of colours, claiming that from these few colours you can mix any colour you want. I have yet to be convinced. My advice is to buy whatever colours you want, but don't compromise on quality – always get the best you can afford at the time.

26 CHOOSING YOUR COLOURS

Shown below is the standard colour range I use. In addition to this basic palette, I use other stronger, brighter colours such as turquoise, which are ideal for painting flowers. I have found over the years that I can mix most of the colours I need from these twelve. The range includes my own ready-made greens: sunlit green, country olive and midnight green.

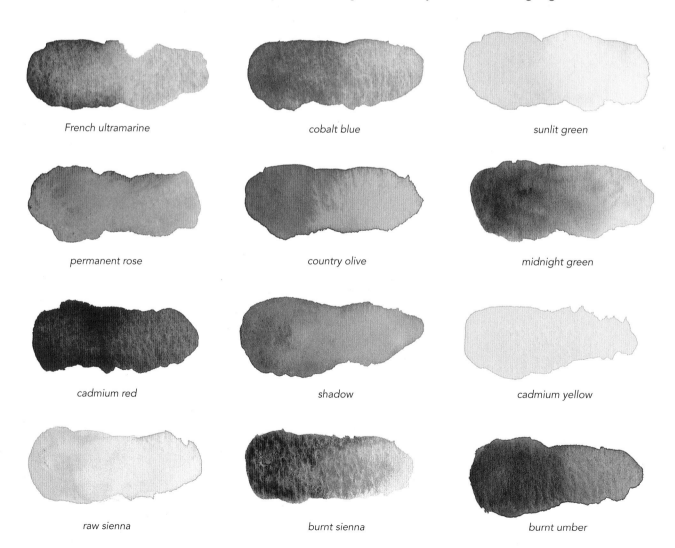

French ultramarine	*cobalt blue*	*sunlit green*
permanent rose	*country olive*	*midnight green*
cadmium red	*shadow*	*cadmium yellow*
raw sienna	*burnt sienna*	*burnt umber*

🪶 **27** LAYING OUT YOUR COLOURS

Personally I prefer to position my colours in my palette in groups; greens
at one end, earth colours in the centre and blues at the other end.

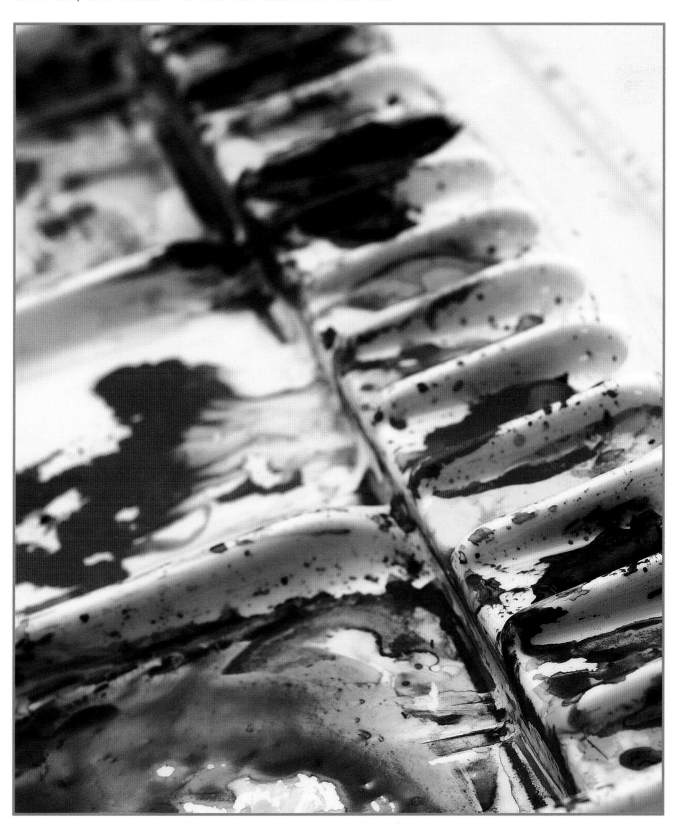

28 MIXING GREYS

Greys can also be mixed from your basic range of colours, as shown here.

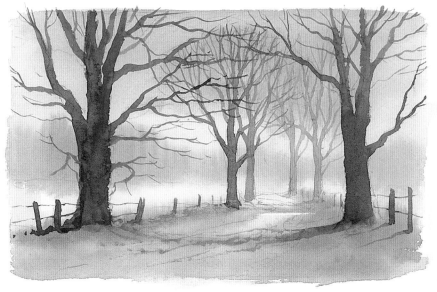

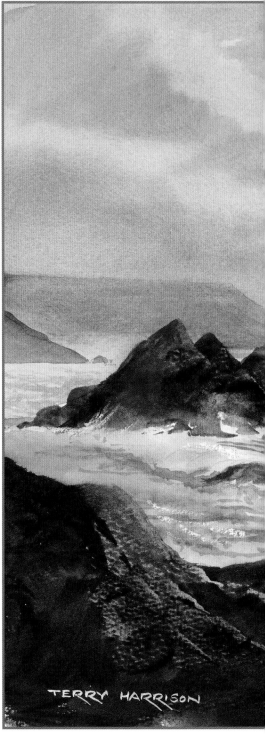

🔺 Two-colour study

This simple painting was achieved using just two colours: permanent rose and midnight green.

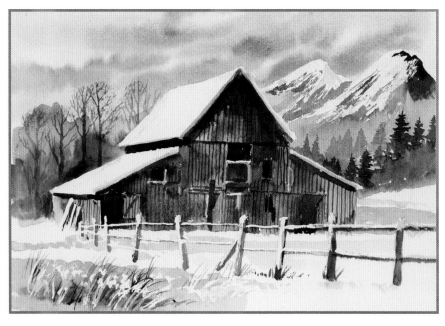

🔺 Snow barn

This snow scene was created using just two colours: ultramarine and burnt umber. For the cool blue-greys, mix more ultramarine than burnt umber. The darks are an even mix of both colours. The warm shades are burnt umber with less ultramarine.

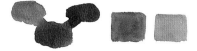

TERRY HARRISON

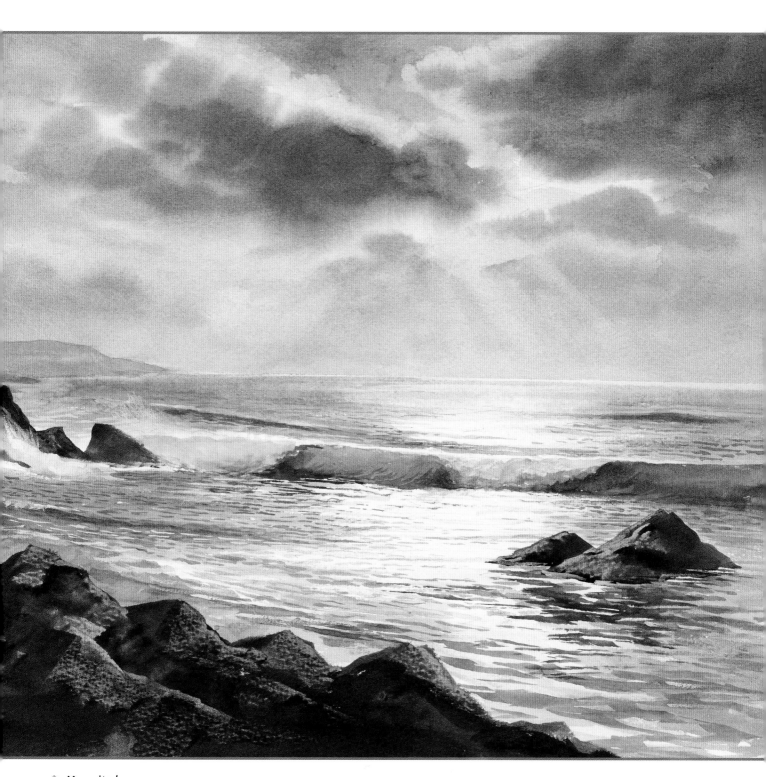

⬆ Moonlit bay

This tonal seascape was painted using only two colours: burnt umber and ultramarine, mixed together to create grey. A dark grey or almost black was achieved by mixing the two colours with only a little water, then the lighter tones were mixed with more water to dilute the colours. The texture of the rocks in the foreground was achieved by scraping the paint away using a plastic card (see page 104).

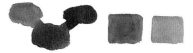

29 NEVER USE BLACK

You often hear the expression 'never use black'. There is a reason for this: black tends to dominate a painting and is a dull, dead colour. You can mix the dark colours you need from your basic range of colours, and by varying the mixes, you can create interesting rather than dead colours.

30 USING READY-MADE GREENS

To mix a successful green, you would need at least two or three different colours. There is a general rule in watercolour painting that if you mix three or four colours, the painting becomes muddy. If you buy a ready-made green, it is a fresher colour and you can treat it as one colour, and add a second and a third colour without the result becoming muddy.

The painting below and the one opposite were both done with my three ready-made greens: midnight green, country olive and sunlit green.

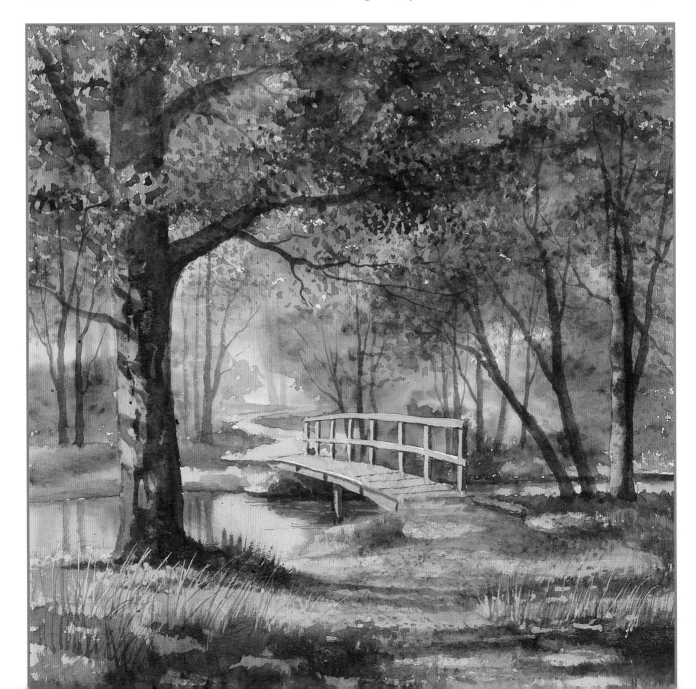

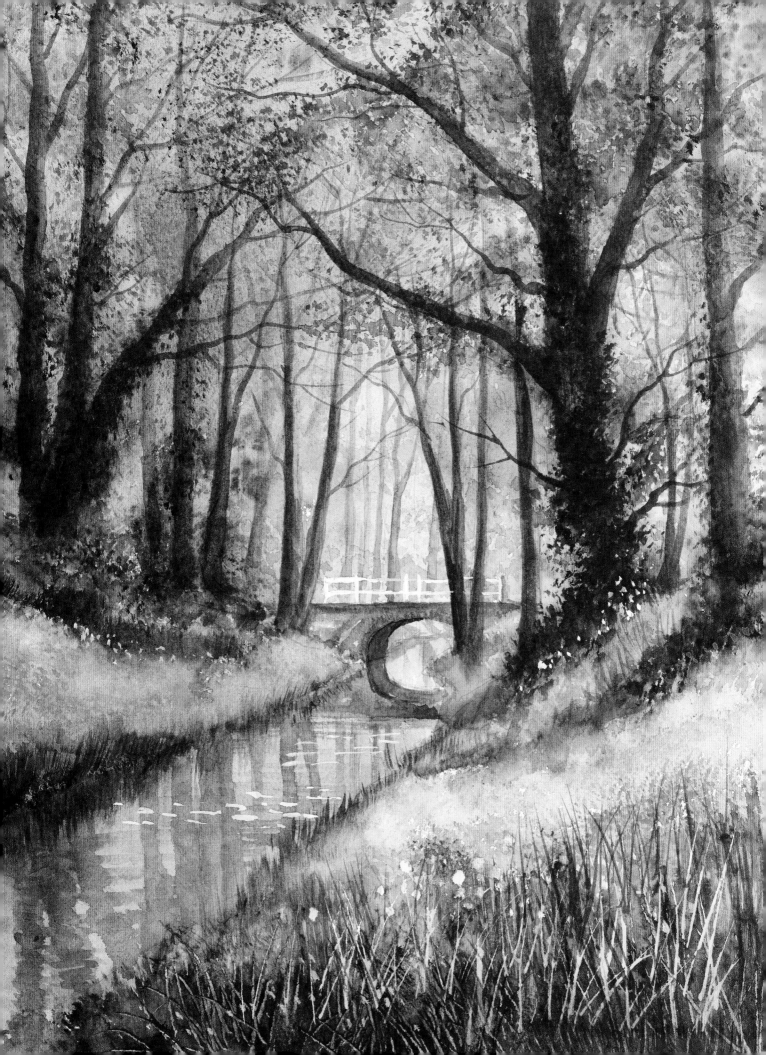

Mixing watercolours

Paint consistency seems to be the biggest hurdle to overcome when you are starting to paint in watercolour. There is no magic formula for getting this right; it comes with experience. It is worth taking the time to practise and experiment with different mixes.

31 ADD PAINT TO WATER, NOT WATER TO PAINT

If you add water to the paint in your palette, you can end up with a very watery mix. If you then need a stronger mix, you will need to start again. Instead, follow the steps shown here.

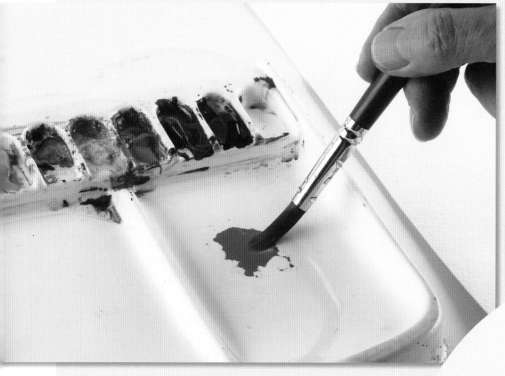

1 Put a damp brush into neat paint and place it in the palette.

2 This will make a strong, solid brushstroke.

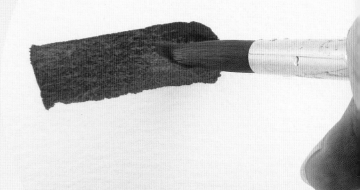

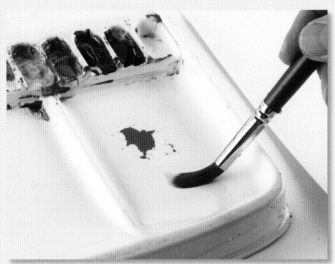

3 Wash the brush and place a little clean water on a clean part of the palette.

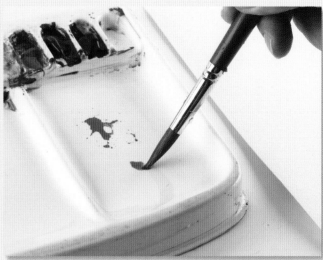

4 Now pick up a little of the neat paint and add it to the water to make a weaker mix.

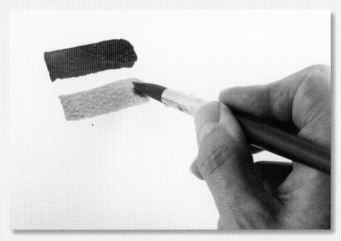

5 Now the brush will make a paler mark.

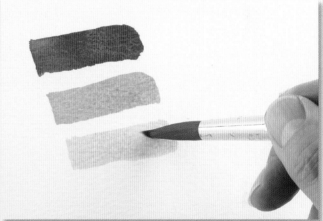

6 You can repeat this process several times, and you will end up with several different options in your palette, from the original strong mix to various weaker tints.

32 TRYING OUT THE MIX

Before using a paint mix in your painting, always try it out first on scrap paper or at the edge of the painting, to see what kind of mark it makes.

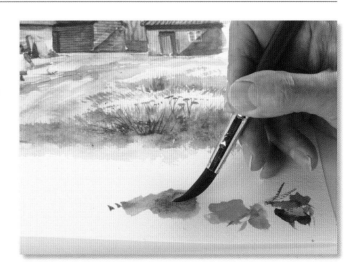

♣ 33 DRYING YOUR BRUSH ON KITCHEN PAPER

Sometimes a paint mix seems right in the palette, but when you apply it to the paper it is too wet to create the type of effect you want. In most cases, the brush is simply overloaded.

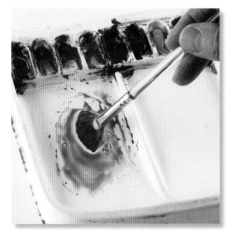

1 Here I make a strong mix of green in the palette, which I want to use with my fan gogh brush to paint grasses.

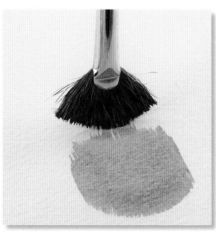

2 When I attempt to flick up the brush to create the effect of grasses, the paint is too wet and fills in the shape.

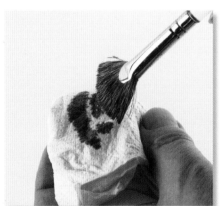

3 Instead of starting again, I remove excess wet paint from the brush by dabbing it on kitchen paper.

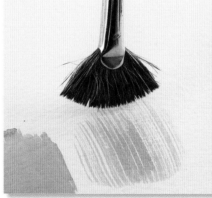

4 The grass effect works perfectly with the drier brush.

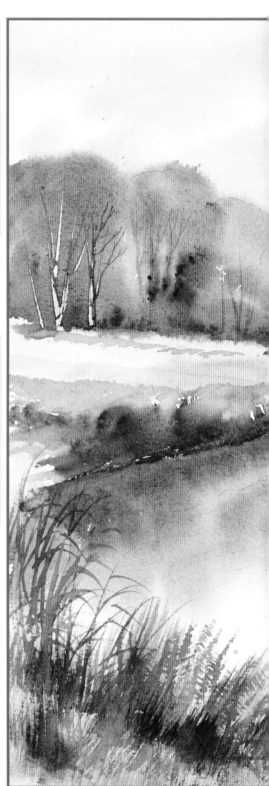

➤ *River bank grasses*
Having less paint in your brush prevents the brushstroke from flooding together, creating a solid wash. Less paint in your brush creates a finer grass effect.

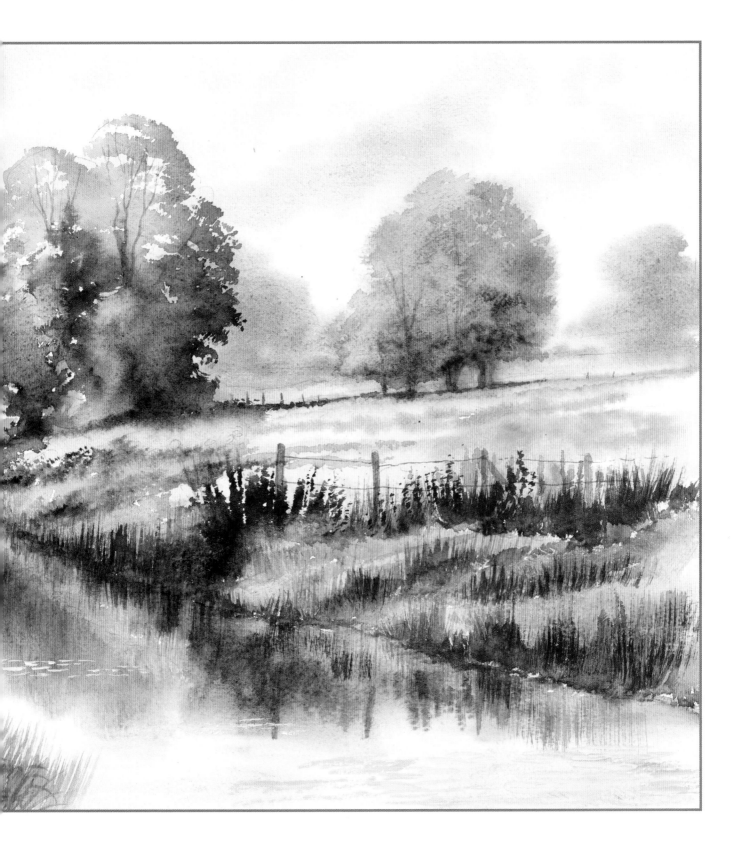

Techniques

Some people think that watercolour is a tricky medium, but really the trick is to learn the right techniques to use with the paints and brushes. Learn the techniques shown here and you should be able to tackle any watercolour landscape. I shall also share with you some of the tips I have developed over the years of painting and teaching.

Washes

Painting a wash might seem simple, as it generally involves just one colour and a big brush, but it can easily go wrong if you use the wrong paint consistency or an unsuitable brush.

34 APPLYING A FLAT WASH

Always mix enough colour so that you do not need to mix more while painting, as a flat wash needs to be applied quickly and smoothly. The painting board should slope down towards you so that the paint will run down slightly to create a bead at the bottom.

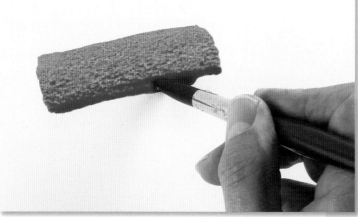

1 Take a large wash brush such as the large detail brush, as this holds plenty of paint. Paint in horizontal strokes, each one lower than the one before it. With each stroke, pick up the bead of paint that forms at the bottom of the wash and use it to paint the next stroke.

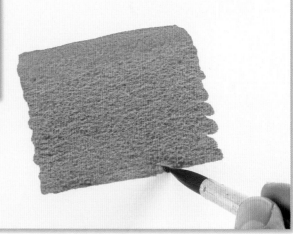

2 Continue extending the wash downwards as shown. Pick up more of the mix from the palette as needed. At the bottom of the wash, use the brush to pick up and remove the bead of paint.

◼ 35 APPLYING A GRADED WASH

A graded wash starts with a strong colour at the top and fades to a paler tint further down as more water is added. The painting board should slope down towards you.

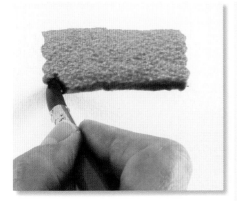

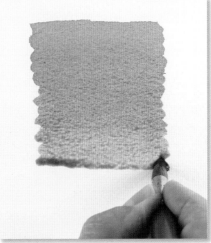

1 Pick up the paint mix from the palette with a large wash brush. Paint in horizontal strokes from the top downwards. A bead of paint should form at the bottom of the wash.

2 Pick up clean water and mix it into the colour on the palette. Feed this into the bead at the bottom of the wash as you paint the next stroke.

3 Continue adding water. At the bottom of the wash, pick up the bead.

◼ 36 APPLYING A VARIEGATED WASH

A variegated wash starts with one colour and merges into another. It should be left to dry on a slope, as it was painted. This allows the colours to continue merging.

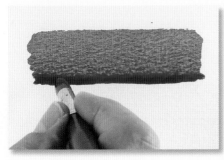

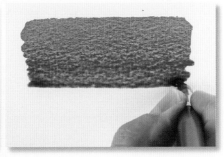

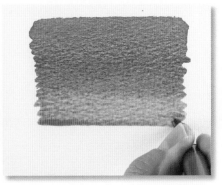

1 Start with one colour. Make sure there is an even bead at the bottom.

2 Clean the brush, pick up the second colour and merge it into the bead. The second colour merges into the first as you continue to paint horizontal strokes down the paper.

3 Wash the brush again and pick up the clean second colour from the palette so that the second colour appears unmixed at the bottom of the wash.

Wet into wet

To achieve this technique, both washes must be wet. If you are applying wet paint into a semi-wet background, the paint you are applying will not flow smoothly into the first colour, but will create unwanted effects such as 'cauliflowers' (see page 62).

37 DROPPING IN A SECOND COLOUR

It may sound obvious, but make sure the first colour is still wet on the paper when you drop in the second.

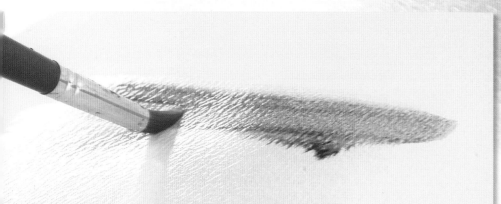

1 Wet the paper first. This slows down the drying time of the first colour so that you have plenty of time to work before the paint dries. Paint on the first colour, here a sky blue.

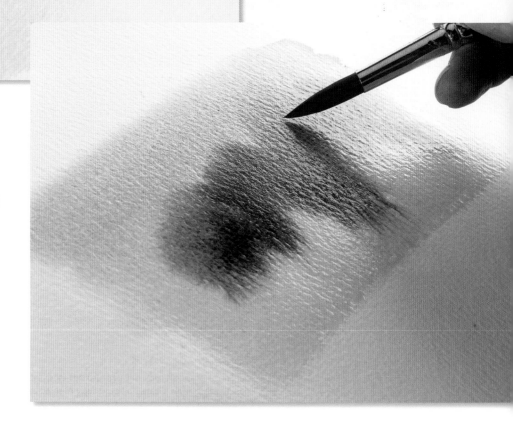

2 Pick up the second colour and dab it on to the paper on top of the first. The second colour spreads into the first, creating a soft, cloud-like effect.

38 USING WET INTO WET ON BUILDINGS

Allowing your colours to mix and merge together on your painting rather than in your palette can create a rustic-looking building. The washes are mixed wet into wet and allowed to dry with an uneven, mottled look.

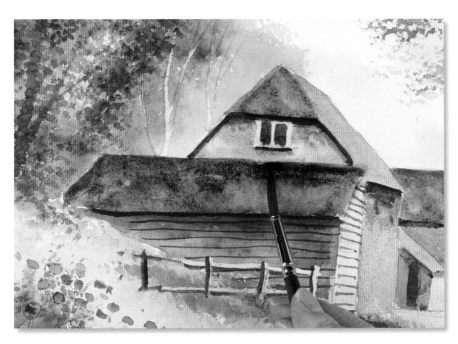

1 Once the roof has dried, wet the area with clean water. Drop in a touch of shadow beneath the ridge with the medium detail brush and burnt sienna.

2 While the roof is still wet, drop in sunlit green to suggest moss towards the bottom.

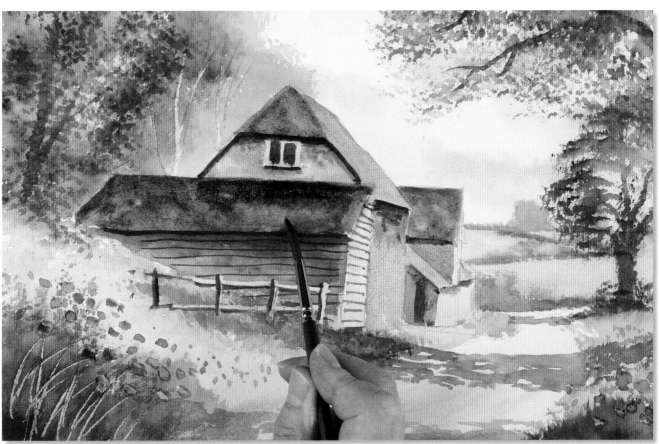

39 USING WET INTO WET TO MAKE RAINCLOUDS

The wet into wet technique is great for clouds, as it produces soft-edged results. It is particularly effective for painting heavy, dark rainclouds just as the rain actually begins.

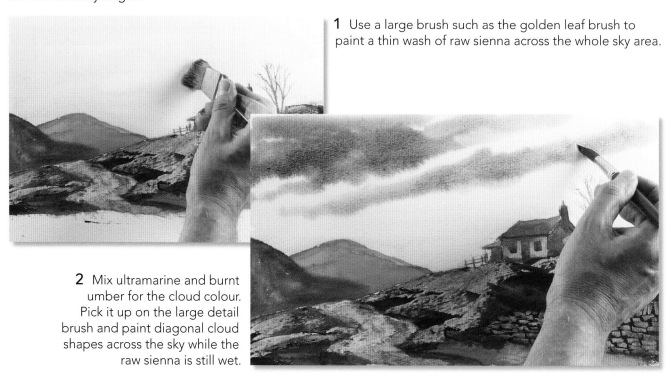

1 Use a large brush such as the golden leaf brush to paint a thin wash of raw sienna across the whole sky area.

2 Mix ultramarine and burnt umber for the cloud colour. Pick it up on the large detail brush and paint diagonal cloud shapes across the sky while the raw sienna is still wet.

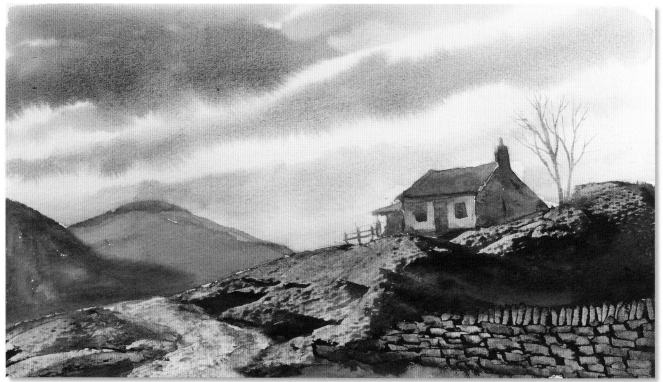

3 Allow the painting to dry naturally. The clouds will continue softening into the background sky colour as the paint dries.

Wet on dry

This technique is suitable for adding detail to a painting. If the background colour is still wet, the colour you are adding will bleed into it, creating unwanted wet into wet effects.

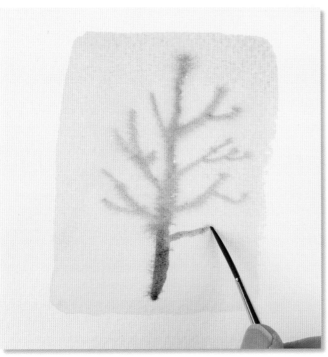

Here a tree is painted into a wet background, causing it to spread and soften, losing detail and clarity.

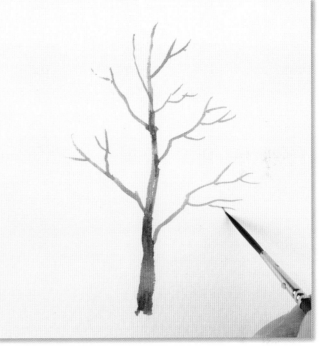

Here the tree is painted with the same half-rigger brush, but on a dry background, which allows for a more controlled, detailed technique.

40 PAINTING ON TOP OF DRIED PAINT

If you allow the background colour to dry thoroughly before applying a second colour, the paint will make clear, hard lines instead of spreading and merging as in the wet into wet technique.

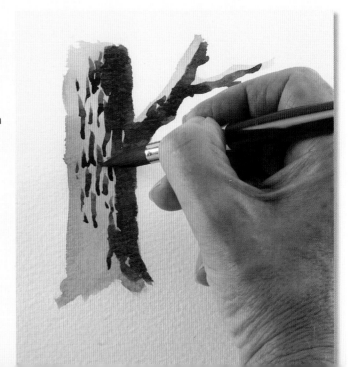

Dry brushwork

This technique can be used to create interesting textures. The paint is picked up on a 'thirsty' brush which is only slightly damp, not wet. The brush is dragged across the surface of Rough paper, where it leaves a speckled effect. You need to keep using kitchen paper to soak up the excess water from the brush as you paint.

41 PAINTING TEXTURE ON TREE BARK

This painting shows how effective the dry brush technique is when painting on tree trunks. The detail was created by the dry brush so don't over-wet the brush. Make sure the surface is dry before you begin.

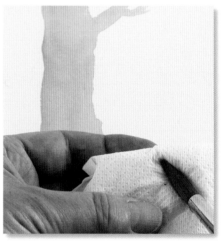

1 Paint the tree trunk with an initial wash, and allow it to dry. Wash the brush with clean water, then dab it on kitchen paper to soak up the excess water.

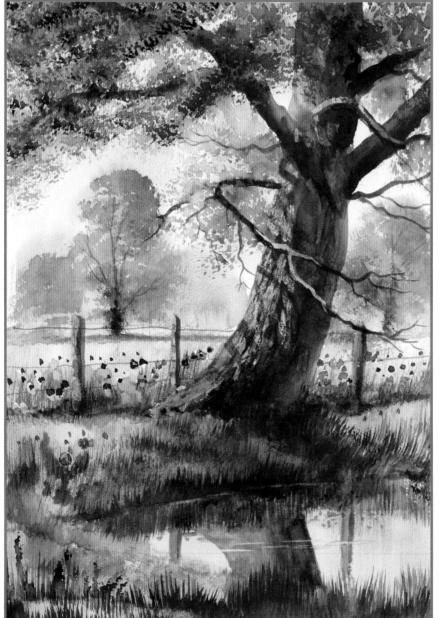

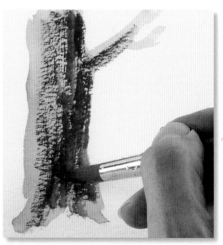

2 Load the brush with the second colour and drag it over the surface of the paper on top of the dried wash, to create a speckled effect. You can then darken the shaded side further.

Summertime walk

In this painting, masking fluid was used on the tree trunk to create a dappled sunlight effect. The foliage on the main tree in the foreground was stippled with the golden leaf brush, and the individual leaves were added using the large detail brush. Dry brushwork was used to create the texture of the weathered wood on the stile.

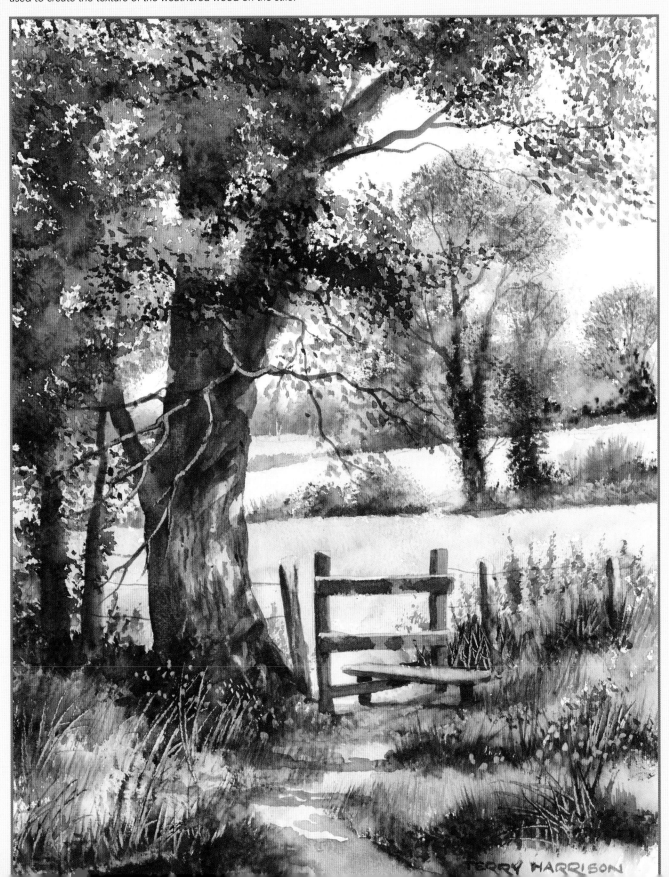

TERRY HARRISON

Glazing

Glazing is applying a wash of colour over whole areas of a dried painting. The wash must be thin enough to be transparent.

42 CREATING A SUNSET USING GLAZING

This woodland scene was painted in grey and brown tones, and then glazed with bright colours to create a sunset.

The original painting.

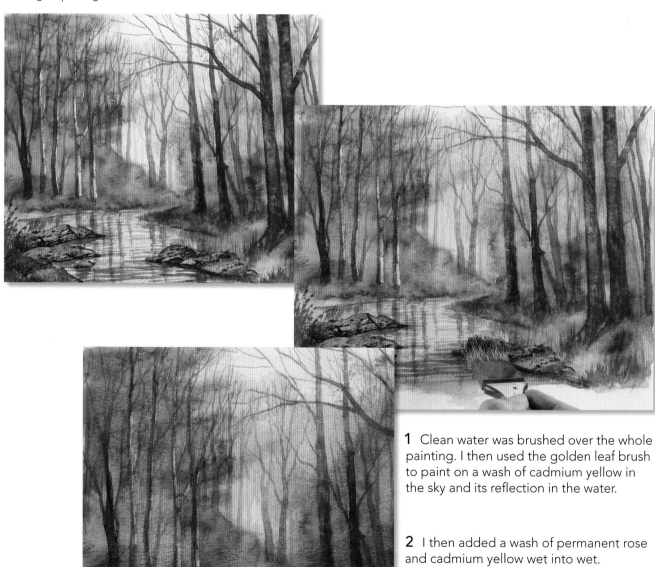

1 Clean water was brushed over the whole painting. I then used the golden leaf brush to paint on a wash of cadmium yellow in the sky and its reflection in the water.

2 I then added a wash of permanent rose and cadmium yellow wet into wet.

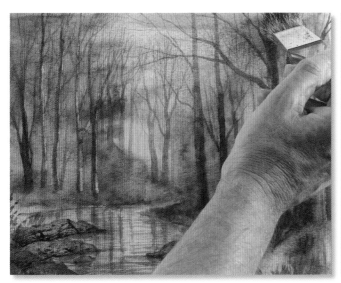

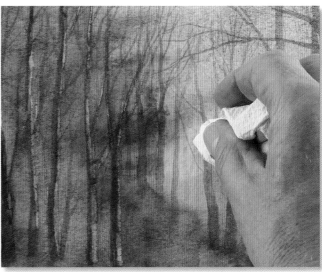

3 I added a glaze of permanent rose at the top of the sky and in the water.

4 Then I lifted out a bright patch in the sky using kitchen paper.

The finished, glazed painting.

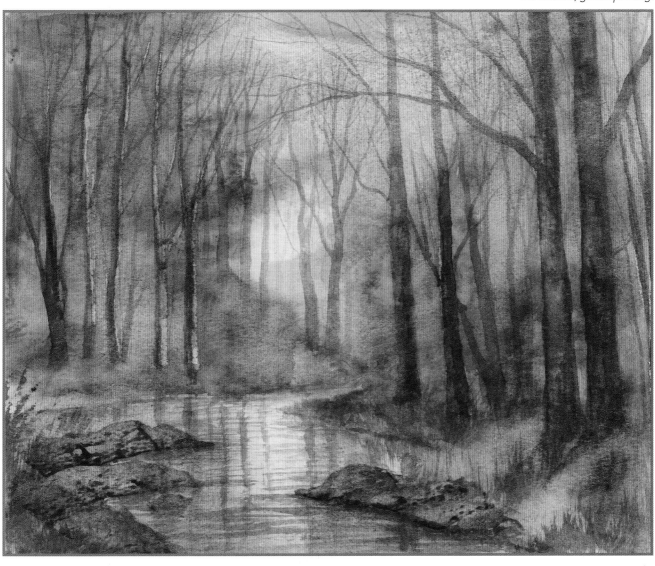

Leabharlanna Poiblí Chathair Bhaile Átha Cliath
Dublin City Public Libraries

Masking

Masking is all about keeping certain parts of the paper white, allowing you to paint freely over the masked area.

When using masking fluid, do not use it on damp paper, as it soaks into the paper and dries. When you remove it, it tears the paper surface.

Do not leave masking fluid on for longer than two or three days, as it becomes too hard and is difficult to remove. The same thing can happen if you dry the masking fluid with a hairdryer.

43 PROTECTING YOUR BRUSH

Masking fluid can ruin your good brushes. To avoid this, wet the brush and rub it in ordinary soap before dipping it in the masking fluid. The masking fluid will then wash out easily when you have finished using it. If masking fluid dries on your brush, washing with soap simply will not remove it, but you can clean the brush with lighter fluid.

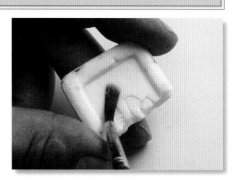

44 APPLYING MASKING FLUID WITH A BRUSH

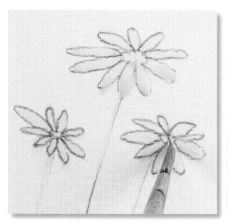

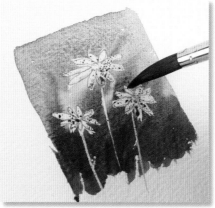

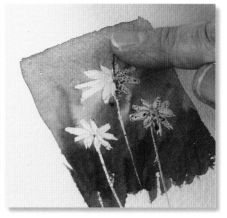

1 Brush on the masking fluid where you want the paper to stay white.

2 Wait for it to dry naturally, then paint your colours over the top.

3 Allow the paints to dry, then rub off the masking fluid with a clean finger.

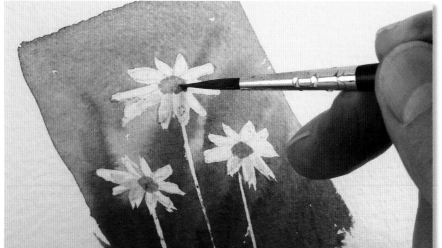

4 You can then paint another colour on to the white areas. I have added pale ultramarine shading and cadmium yellow centres to these daisies.

🌑 45 MASKING OUT SNOWY BRANCHES

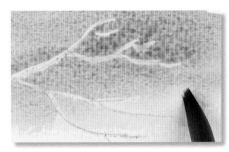

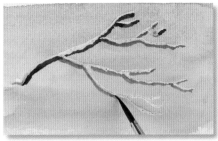

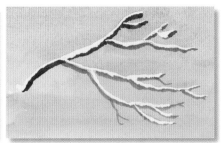

The finished branch.

1 Paint the branch with masking fluid on the masking fluid brush and allow it to dry. Paint over it with a wash of ultramarine and the large detail brush.

2 Mix ultramarine and burnt umber and use the small detail brush to run this colour over the underside of the branch. The top part will be snow. Allow to dry and rub off the masking fluid.

🌑 46 USING A RULING PEN TO APPLY MASKING FLUID

When using a ruling pen, do not have the gap in the nib too wide, or the masking fluid will come out in blobs.

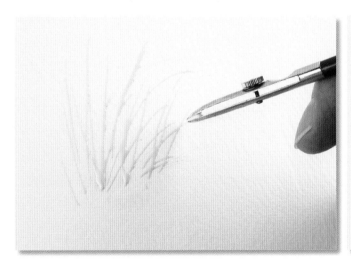

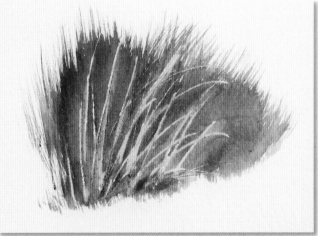

1 Load the ruling pen by dipping it in the masking fluid. Do not overload it or the fluid will flood out. Paint the grasses.

2 When the masking fluid is dry, flick up grasses using the darker green mix. Allow to dry, then rub off the masking fluid. You can now apply a lighter green mix and some yellow to the white areas.

🞄47 MASKING USING THE EDGE OF A PIECE OF CARD

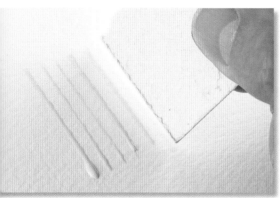

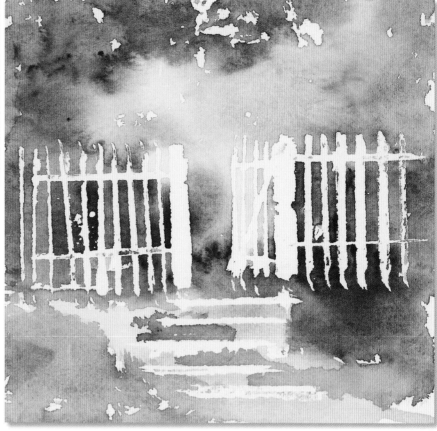

1 Dip the edge of the piece of card in a saucer of masking fluid. Apply it to the paper as shown to create a fence.

2 Allow the masking fluid to dry and then proceed with your painting. When the painting is dry, remove the masking fluid. You can now add a wash to the white areas.

🞄48 APPLYING MASKING FLUID BY SPATTERING

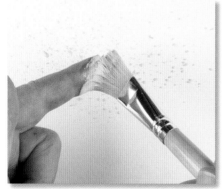

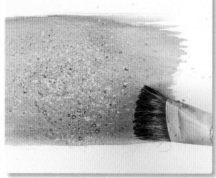

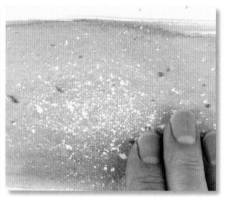

1 Use a cheap bristle brush for this purpose. Put masking fluid in a saucer and dip in the brush. Rub the brush against your finger to flick spatters of masking fluid onto the paper.

2 When the masking fluid is dry, paint a wash over it.

3 Allow the paint to dry, then rub off the masking fluid with your fingers to reveal the speckled effect.

🍂 49 APPLYING MASKING FLUID USING A COLOUR SHAPER

  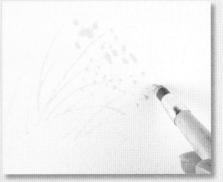

1 Use the larger end of the colour shaper to paint grass and stalks with masking fluid.

2 Dot in flower heads with the same end of the colour shaper.

3 Use the other end of the colour shaper to dot in smaller flower heads for variety. Allow the masking fluid to dry.

4 Use the large detail to paint country olive over the dried masking fluid. Allow to dry.

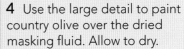

5 Rub off the masking fluid with clean fingers then paint over the grasses and stalks with the small detail brush and sunlit green. Finally paint the flower heads in cadmium red and cadmium yellow.

50 APPLYING MASKING FLUID USING A SPONGE

You can use a synthetic sponge but the best ones for creating texture are the natural ones, as synthetic sponges are often too smooth.

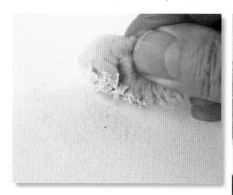

1 Wet a sponge and squeeze out all the excess moisture. Dip it in a saucer of masking fluid and dab it on to the paper.

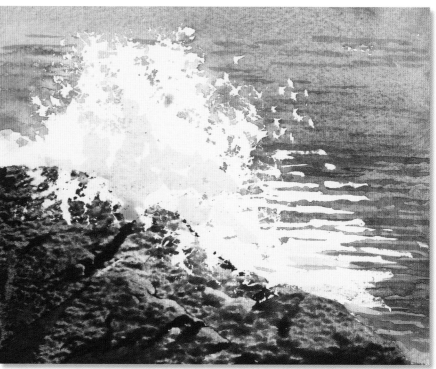

2 Once the masking fluid is dry, paint the sea and the rocks. When the paint is dry, rub off the masking fluid to reveal the white spray area. You can shade this with a little cobalt blue.

51 USING A PAPER MASK TO PAINT HEDGEROWS

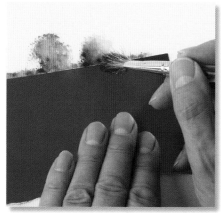

1 Take a piece of magazine type paper (glossy, coated paper) with a straight edge and hold it firmly on your watercolour paper. Paint a hedgerow and bushes just above the paper mask as shown.

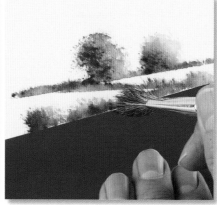

2 Carefully move the mask and change the angle, then paint another hedgerow coming further forwards. Continue in this way.

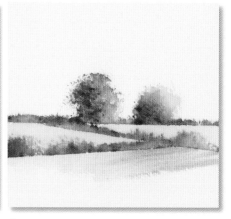

3 Fill in the fields between the hedgerows with different colours, making the colours warmer as they come further forwards, to create the effect of a patchwork of fields stretching into the distance.

52 APPLYING MASKING FLUID USING KITCHEN PAPER

Kitchen paper can be used to apply masking fluid to trees, creating the effect of snow clinging to branches.

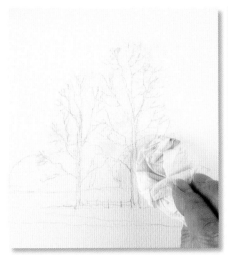

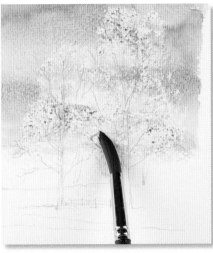

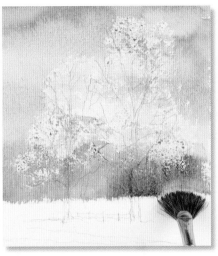

1 Draw the scene. Dip a scrunched-up piece of kitchen paper in masking fluid and dab it onto the trees, gently tapping over the drawing. Allow to dry.

2 Use the large detail brush and ultramarine to paint the sky over the masking fluid.

3 While the sky is wet, use the fan gogh brush to paint a grey mix of ultramarine and burnt umber in the lower part of the sky.

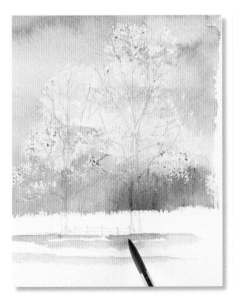

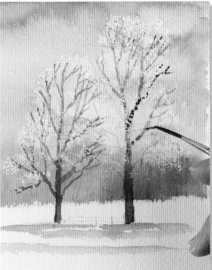

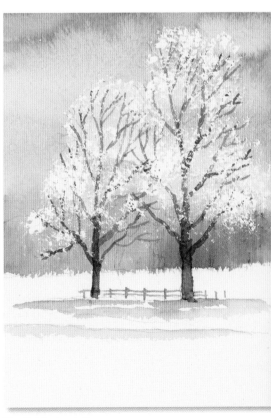

4 Use the large brush and ultramarine to paint shade on the snow in the foreground. Allow to dry.

5 Use the half-rigger with a dark mix of burnt umber and ultramarine to paint in the trunks and branches. Allow to dry, then rub off the masking fluid.

The finished painting.

Lifting out

Because watercolour is water soluble, you can re-wet the paint and remove it in many different ways, for example with a sponge, kitchen paper or a damp brush. Be cautious, as some paints are staining colours and are more difficult to remove. To be on the safe side, practise lifting out paint on a separate piece of paper.

53 LIFTING OUT USING A BRUSH WITH A PAPER MASK

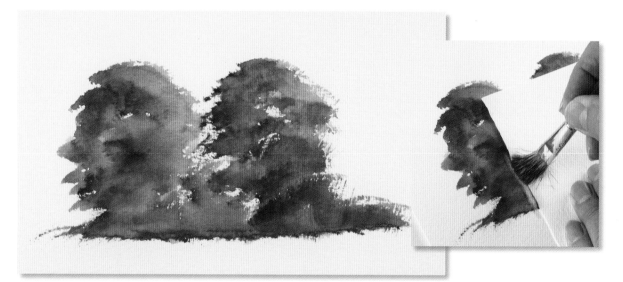

1 Paint tree shapes down to the ground and leave to dry. Take a stiff bristle brush, wet it and dab it on kitchen paper. Use it along the edge of a paper mask to lift out a trunk shape.

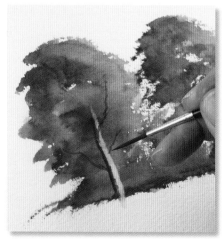

2 Take a thin brush such as a half-rigger and paint a shadow down one side of the trunk, and branches.

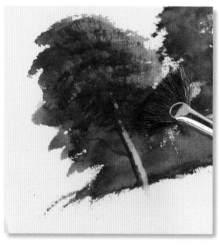

3 Use a fan brush and the darker green to stipple texture for foliage.

54 USING A DAMP BRUSH

Allow the painting to dry. Wet a flat brush and remove excess water on kitchen paper. Now use the straight line of the brush end to lift out a trunk and branches from the painted foliage background. You can go on to add shade as with the other tree.

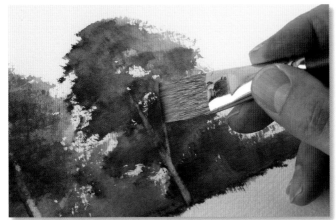

55 USING KITCHEN PAPER

Sometimes an object you have painted comes out too dark; for instance, a tree can look too dominant and too far forwards. To repair this effect, allow the trunk to dry, then wet it with clean water on a brush to loosen the colour. Blot the wet trunk with kitchen paper to lift out colour.

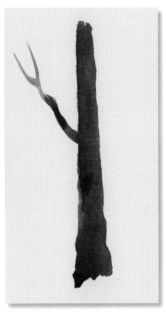

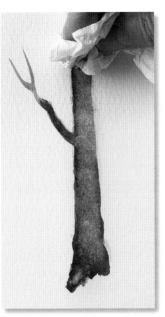

56 LIFTING OUT WITH A MAGIC WATERCOLOUR ERASER

A few years ago when I was teaching in the US, I was shown a fantastic tip for removing unwanted watercolour. It was a small block of white plastic foam impregnated with a cleaning solution, called a 'magic eraser'. These are now available in most supermarkets in the household cleaning section. You simply wet the sponge with clean water, then rub it over the dried watercolour, and it will remove the colour, going right back to the paper, as if by magic. Once it is dry, paint can be added on top.

Use the magic watercolour eraser to create a nice faded effect around a painting's edges, as shown right. Wipe the edges with the eraser and then dab with kitchen paper to lift off the colour.

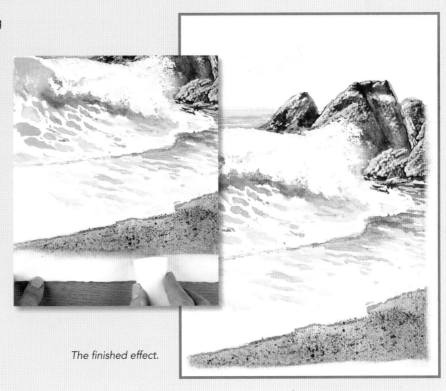

The finished effect.

57 LIFTING OUT THE SUN WITH A MAGIC WATERCOLOUR ERASER

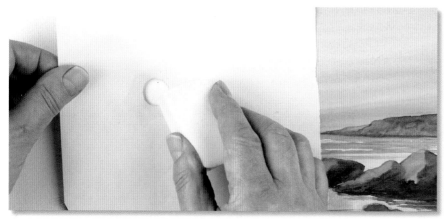

Cut a circular hole in a paper mask the size you need the sun to be. Dip the magic watercolour eraser in water and use it to rub out the colour through the paper mask. Lift out further colour with kitchen paper.

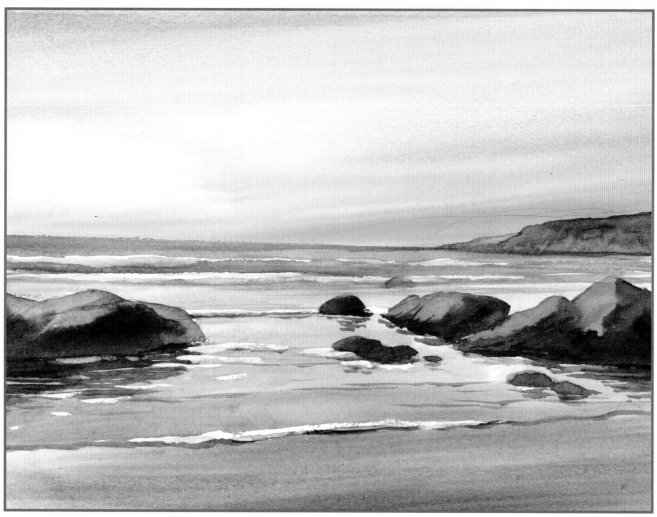

The finished effect.

58 LIFTING OUT TO CREATE SHAFTS OF LIGHT

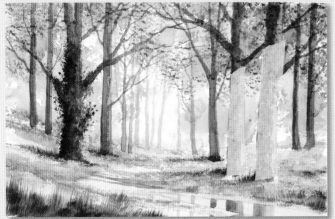

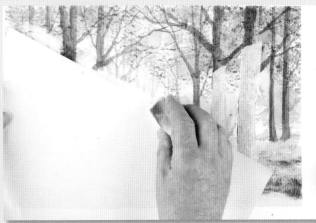

1 Begin by masking the two foreground trees so that the shafts of light will look as though they are behind them.

2 Place a paper mask at an angle where you want the first shaft of light. Sponge along the edge and dab with kitchen paper to lift out colour.

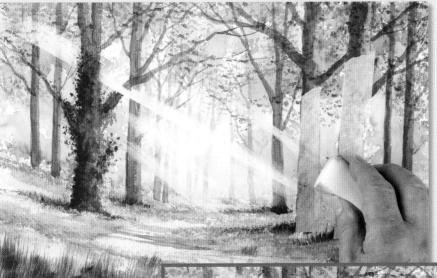

3 Continue freehand, lifting out further shafts of light.

The finished effect. The bluebell wood is now shot through with convincing shafts of sunlight.

Special effects

You do not necessarily need special equipment to produce special effects in watercolour. Many of the effects shown here are created using items that can be found in any home, such as salt, cling film and candle wax. You can buy specialist materials such as texture paste and watercolour ground if you would like to add to your repertoire, but they are not essential.

59 USING SALT TO CREATE TEXTURE

Salt can be used with watercolour to produce some striking textured effects that can be really useful for landscape painting.

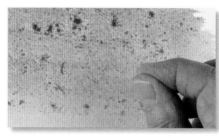 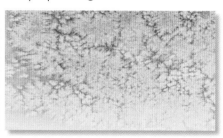

1 Don't use the paint too wet for this technique. Here I have painted on an ultramarine wash. While it is wet, sprinkle on salt. Rock salt works well, but here I have used just ordinary table salt.

2 Leave the salt in place and allow the paint to dry completely, then brush off the salt to reveal the effect.

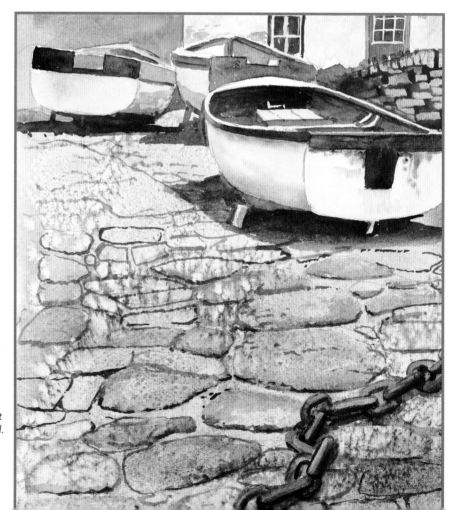

Salt was used to create the weathered effect on the flagstones in the foreground.

🞂60 SPATTERING WITH A FOLIAGE BRUSH

Mask the part of the painting you do not want spattered with spare paper, as shown below. Make a wash of burnt umber, dip the foliage brush in it and use your finger to flick the bristles, spattering paint over the painting – in this case the shingle beach. The finished effect is shown right.

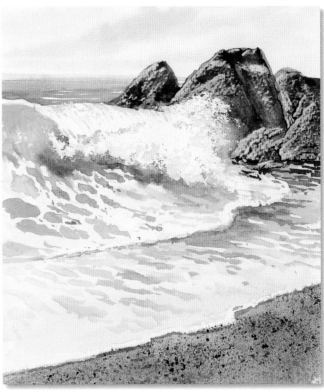

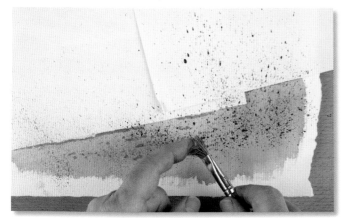

🞂61 USING A CANDLE WAX RESIST TO CREATE SPARKLE ON WATER

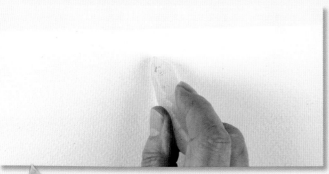

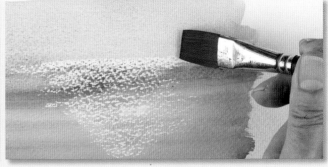

1 Rub white wax candle along the edge of a paper mask to create the sparkling area on the water.

2 Use the 19mm (¾in) flat brush to paint ultramarine over the water and sky areas. Allow to dry.

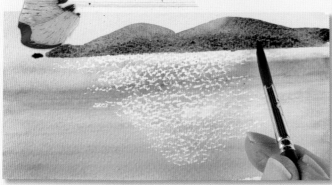

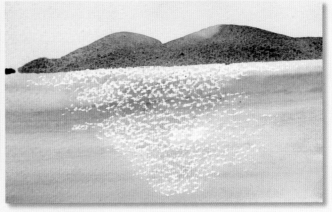

3 Mix ultramarine and burnt umber and use the medium detail brush to paint hills going down to a flat horizon line.

The finished scene.

62 USING TEXTURE PASTE WITH WATERCOLOUR GROUND

Texture paste is usually used with acrylic paint, and watercolour tends to sink into it and go dull. However, you can still use it with watercolour if you coat it with a special watercolour ground first.

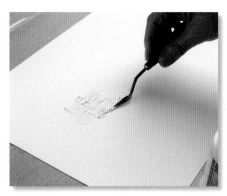
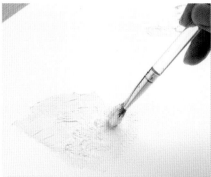

Acrylic texture medium can be applied with a painting knife, as shown far left.

You can also use a stiff brush such as the foliage brush (shown left).

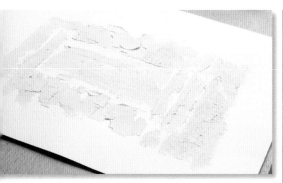

1 I used acrylic texture paste on this doorway scene. I brushed it on and then allowed it to dry.

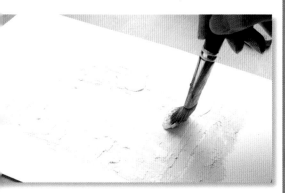

2 Paint watercolour ground over the top of the texture paste with a large brush and allow it to dry. This prevents watercolour paint from sinking into the texture medium and going dull.

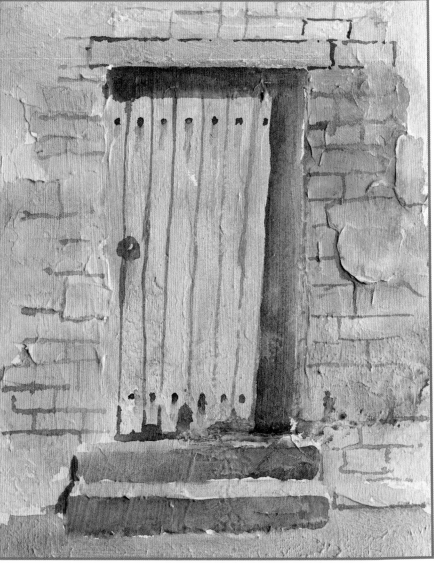

The finished doorway. You can see the full step-by-step process on pages 118 -119.

63 USING CLING FILM TO CREATE PATTERN AND TEXTURE

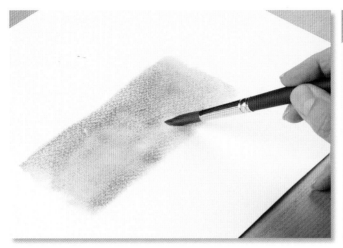

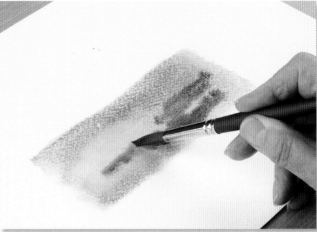

1 Wet the paper and paint on cobalt blue with the large detail brush, then drop in raw sienna wet into wet.

2 While the background is still wet, drop in burnt sienna.

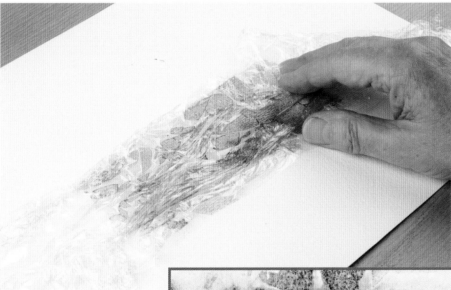

3 Scrunch up a piece of cling film to create texture and push it into the wet paint in places. Allow to dry.

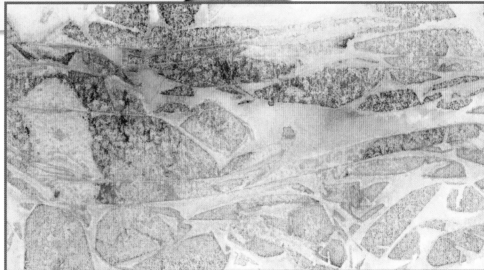

The finished effect.

Troubleshooting

Unwanted hard lines, such as bleedbacks, cauliflowers, backruns and tide lines – call them what you like, they are still a pain. The trick is to know why they happen so you don't make the same mistakes again.

64 AVOIDING HARD LINES

Unwanted hard lines occur if you are attempting a wet into wet effect, but the first wash dries as you are applying the second. The darker cloud colour shown here should have spread softly into the background, but it has dried in unconvincing hard lines. To avoid this, always work while the paint is still wet.

65 AVOIDING THE CAULIFLOWER EFFECT

A cauliflower effect is created if you drop a thinner wash on top of thicker wet paint, as shown here. To avoid this, when working wet into wet, make sure each subsequent paint mix is thicker than the one before it.

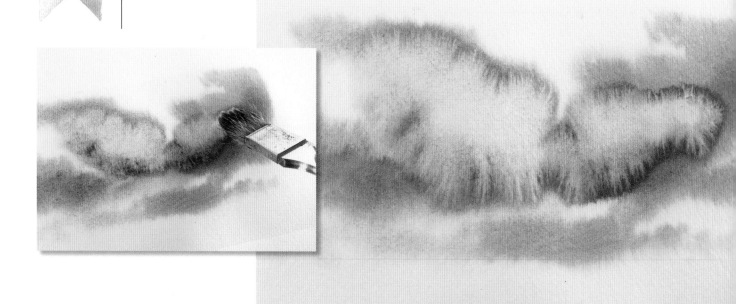

66 REPAIRING CAULIFLOWERS

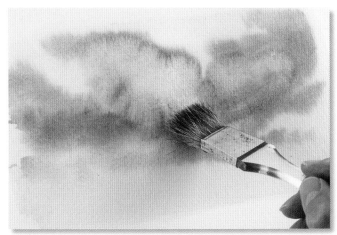

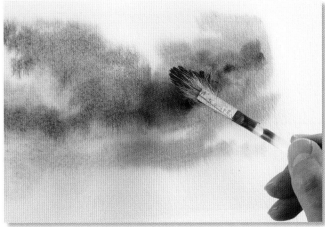

1 When the painting is dry, wet the whole area with clean water. Use the golden leaf brush to agitate the edges of the cloud where it has dried into a cauliflower effect.

2 While the painting is still wet, drop in the ultramarine and burnt umber mix to create dark clouds.

67 REPAIRING UNWANTED HARD LINES

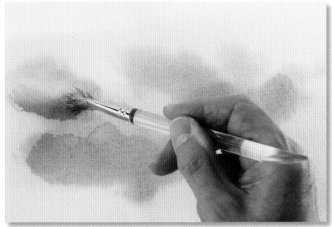

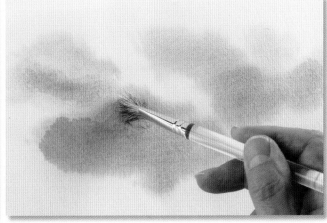

1 Wait until the painting is thoroughly dry. Wet the area that needs repairing and beyond it, so that any paint that you disturb will flow into the wet area.

2 Use the brush to scrub gently around the hard line to remove it.

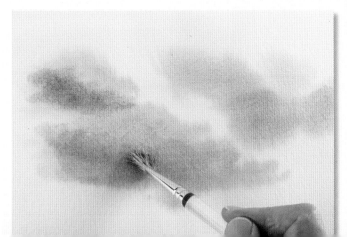

3 Now you can complete the painting of the clouds, working wet into wet. Drop in a mix of ultramarine and burnt umber while the paper is still wet.

⬛ 68 PREVENTING THE PAPER FROM DRYING TOO FAST

If you want to paint wet into wet for a fairly long time, you need the paper to stay wet, as once it starts to dry, it can cause cauliflowers. To keep the painting wet for longer, wet the paper before you begin.

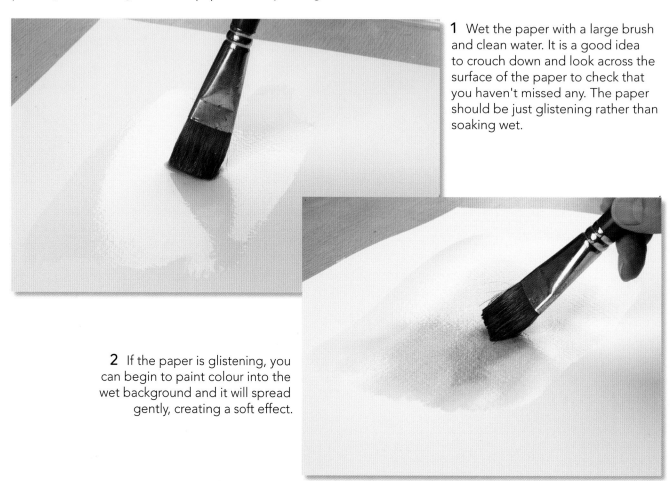

1 Wet the paper with a large brush and clean water. It is a good idea to crouch down and look across the surface of the paper to check that you haven't missed any. The paper should be just glistening rather than soaking wet.

2 If the paper is glistening, you can begin to paint colour into the wet background and it will spread gently, creating a soft effect.

⬛ 69 AVOIDING MAKING THE PAPER TOO WET

If the paper is too wet, either because you put too much water on at the start, or because your paint mixes were too wet, other problems can occur.

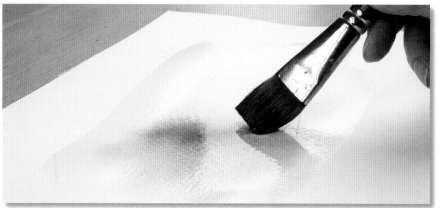

Here the paper was too wet to start with and puddles of water have formed. The paint does not spread evenly and is hard to control. Make sure you wet the paper until it is just glistening, as shown above.

70 PREVENTING COCKLING

If the paper is too wet, it can cockle, as discussed on page 11. One further way to avoid this is to tape the paper down just inside the picture area, rather than round the very edges. If you tape the paper to the board round all its edges, it will expand and cockle when it gets too wet.

Tape just the top of the paper to the board with masking tape. Then tape round the picture area, which will ensure nice, straight edges and will also prevent the paper from cockling as a result of all the wet washes.

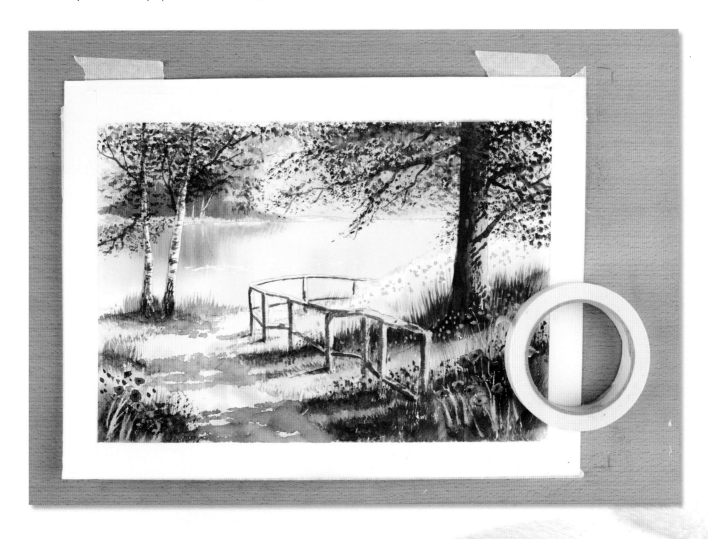

Skies

The general rule when painting landscapes is to paint the sky first. I know I hate rules, but this is a good one! You build a painting from the back to the front, so the order is sky, far distance, middle distance and then foreground.

I use two blues when painting skies: ultramarine and cobalt blue. I tend to use cobalt blue for Mediterranean skies, and ultramarine when painting most other skies.

❀71 PAINTING A CLEAR SKY

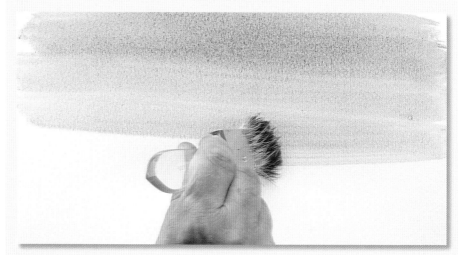

1 Wet the sky area first with clean water and the golden leaf brush. Load the brush evenly with a wash of ultramarine. Start at the top and paint from side to side.

2 As you continue down the paper, the sky gets lighter as there is less colour on the brush. The wet into wet technique disperses any streaks.

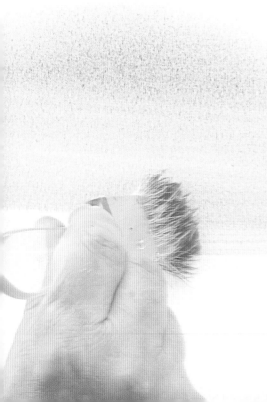

72 LEAVING SPACES FOR CLOUDS

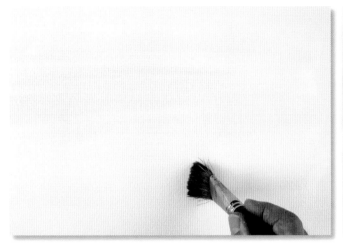

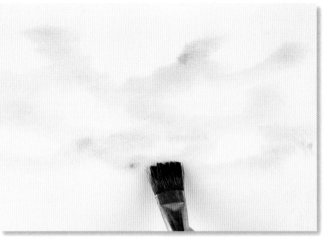

1 Wet the sky area first with the golden leaf brush and clean water, then paint on raw sienna in horizontal strokes.

2 While this is wet, paint on ultramarine, leaving spaces for clouds. Make the clouds smaller at the bottom of the sky to create perspective.

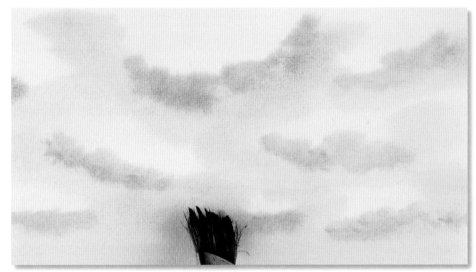

3 Mix ultramarine and burnt umber to make grey and, while the sky is still wet, drop this in beneath the cloud shapes to create shadow. Allow the sky to dry naturally.

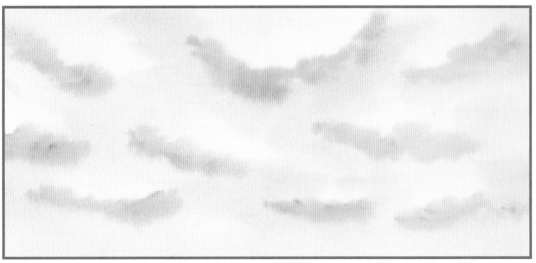

The finished sky.

73 DROPPING IN CLOUDS

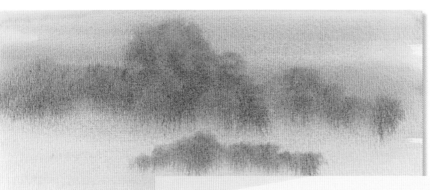

1 Paint the sky wash and while it is wet, drop in a dark mix of burnt umber and ultramarine to create cloud shapes.

2 Use kitchen paper to lift out lighter areas at the tops of the clouds, creating highlights.

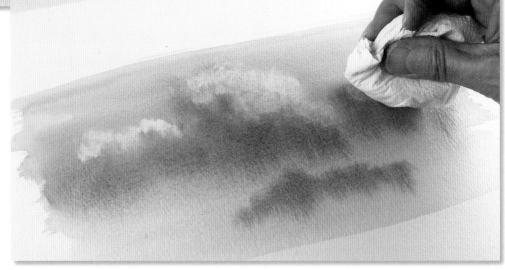

The finished sky.

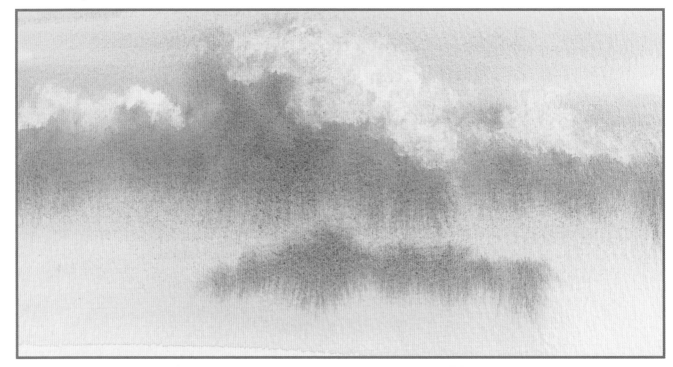

74 CREATING CLOUDS WITH HARD EDGES

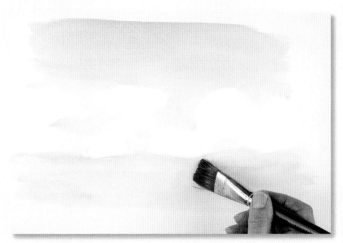

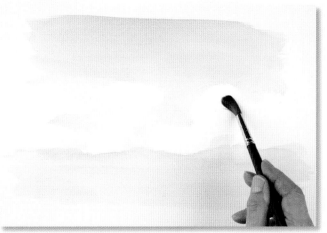

1 Do not wet the sky before beginning to paint. Use the golden leaf brush and ultramarine blue to paint the blue of the sky, leaving spaces for clouds. Allow to dry.

2 Use the large detail brush and clean water to wet the cloud shapes, leaving a dry edge at the top.

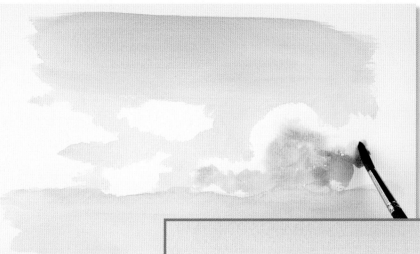

3 Mix ultramarine and burnt umber to make grey and drop this into the wet parts of the clouds. The paint should spread softly into the wet background but stop at the dry parts, leaving the clouds with brightly lit areas. Continue in this way, wetting clouds and dropping in shadow.

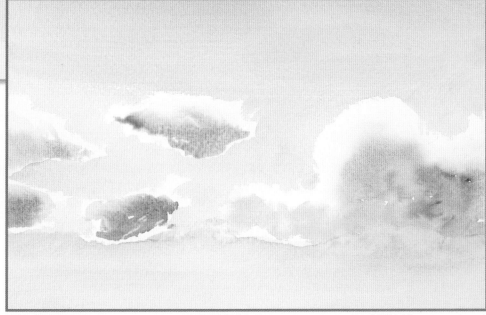

The finished sky.

75 CREATING A WET INTO WET SUNSET

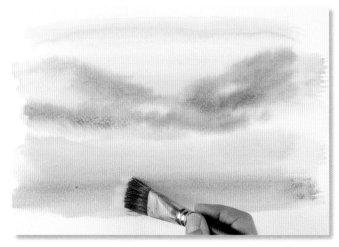

1 Wet the sky area with the golden leaf brush and clean water, then paint cadmium yellow with a little raw sienna across the lower part in horizontal strokes.

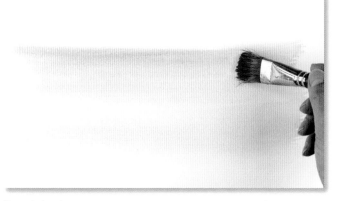

2 While this is wet, paint permanent rose at the top and bottom of the yellow area.

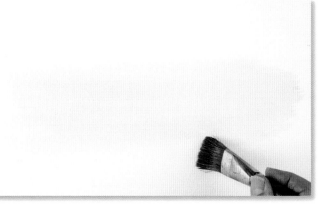

3 Paint horizontal strokes of cobalt blue at the top of the sky and bring this down into the wet pink.

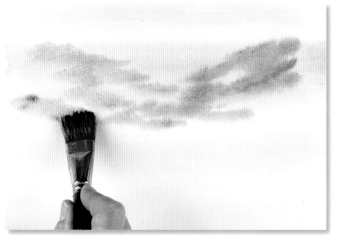

4 Still working into the wet background, paint clouds with shadow colour.

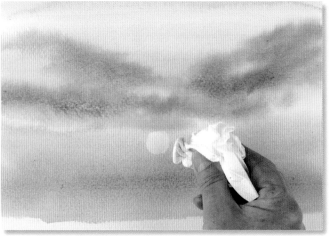

5 Mix cadmium yellow with permanent rose and paint this at the bottom of the wet sky.

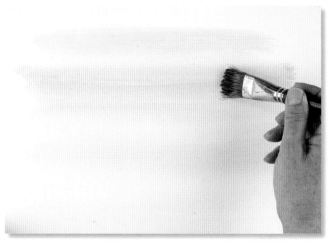

6 Wrap a coin in kitchen paper and use this to lift out a circle for the sun.

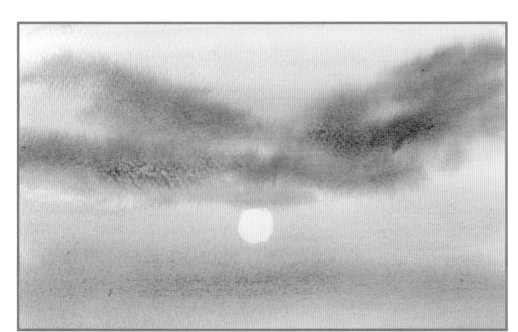

The finished sunset.

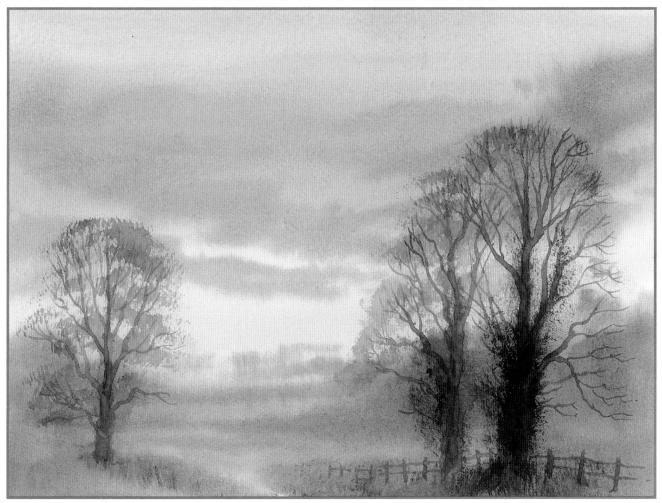

This is another example of a sunset. The sky and the background were painted wet into wet, then allowed to dry. The trees and details were painted on to the dried surface. The sunset is cadmium yellow with cadmium red on the horizon and permanent rose above this, fading into cobalt blue to create a purple.

Distance

To create distance in a painting, you need to dilute your colours to make them paler, and also make them bluer or cooler.

▶ 76 USING COLOUR TO CREATE AN AERIAL PERSPECTIVE

In this example, I have used a pale wash of ultramarine blue for the far distant hill, then a warmer mix of ultramarine and burnt umber for the next hill forwards, then a stronger mix of the same colours for the nearer hills. The warm colour in the foreground is a reflection of the sky colour.

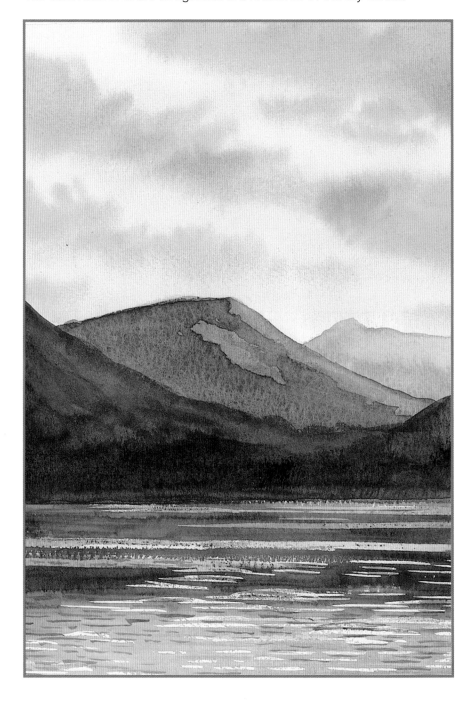

77 CREATING AERIAL PERSPECTIVE THROUGH TONE

The overall atmosphere of this painting is cool and misty, but the depth and distance are created by tone. The trees in the far distance are painted with a very pale, watered down mix. By adding more pigment to the mix, I have made the trees in the middle distance stronger and darker. The tree in the foreground is very strong and dark in tone, almost like a silhouette.

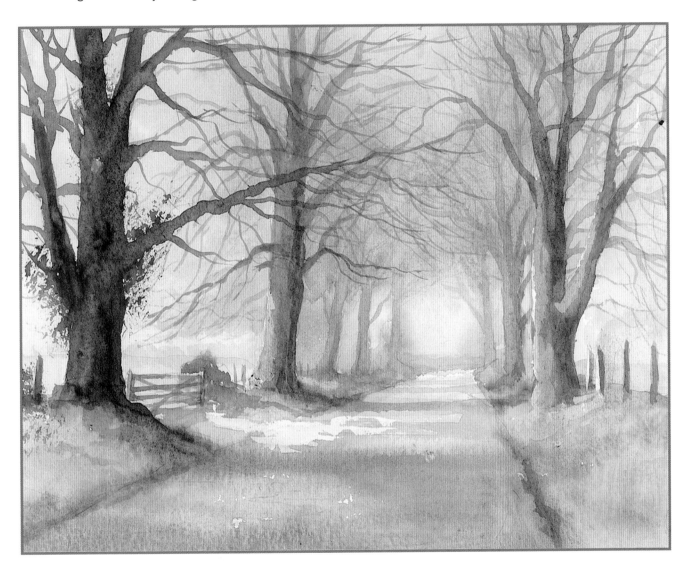

Pearse Street Branch
Brainse Sráid Piarsach
Tel: 6744888

Fields

Note that the colours in distant fields should be paler and bluer, and the fields should be smaller. This will enhance the sense of distance. Add different colours to each individual field to create a patchwork effect.

78 PAINTING SIMPLE FIELDS

The hedgerows are created by masking (see page 52).

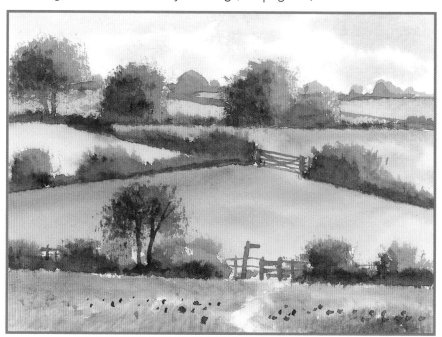

79 PAINTING FIELDS TO ADD DEPTH

In the painting opposite I have used the fields to help create a sense of distance in the painting by having the fields in the far distance small and pale and bluish in tone. The fields in the foreground are much larger and stronger in colour. The fields are painted obliquely, creating a criss-cross shape that leads the eye into the distance, and the farm track also leads into the painting, disappearing and reappearing in among the fields. The addition of the buildings establishes the scale of the scene.

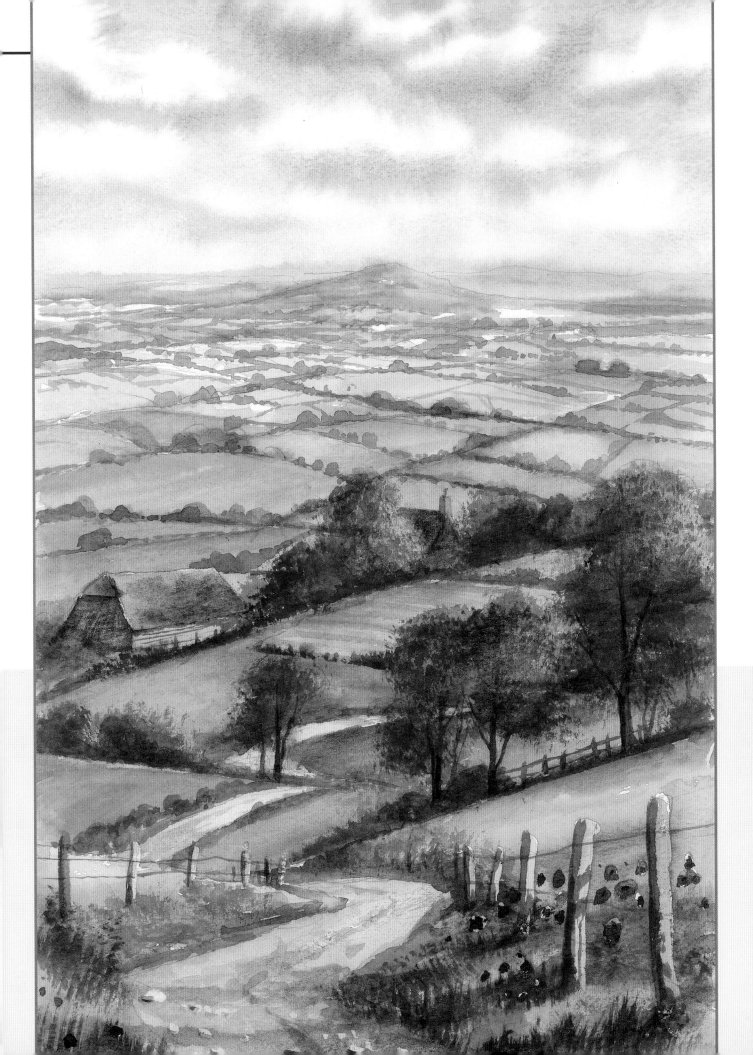

Trees

Trees are a vital part of the landscape and interesting trees can make a big difference to a scene. I prefer to create an impression rather than slavishly reproduce every detail, but it is still important to learn how to paint different trees and the way they change with the seasons.

80 PAINTING MISTY TREES

The key to painting misty trees is to use the wet into wet technique. Paint the sky and the background colour in first, and drop the trees into the wet paint so the paint dissolves into the background colour. Scrape out the white trunks with the end of a px (clear acrylic resin) brush handle.

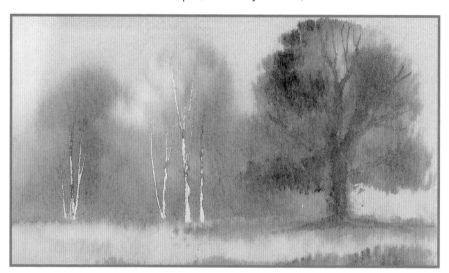

81 VARYING THE TONE OF TREES TO ADD DEPTH

In this painting, trees create a sense of depth and you are drawn deep into the landscape. The tree in the foreground is the largest and the strongest in colour. From the foreground to the middle distance, then to the far distance, the trees reduce in size and become paler in tone and cooler in colour.

Winter walk

Placing the dog walker in the lane allows the viewer to pause for a moment instead of being drawn deep into the distance (see also page 127).

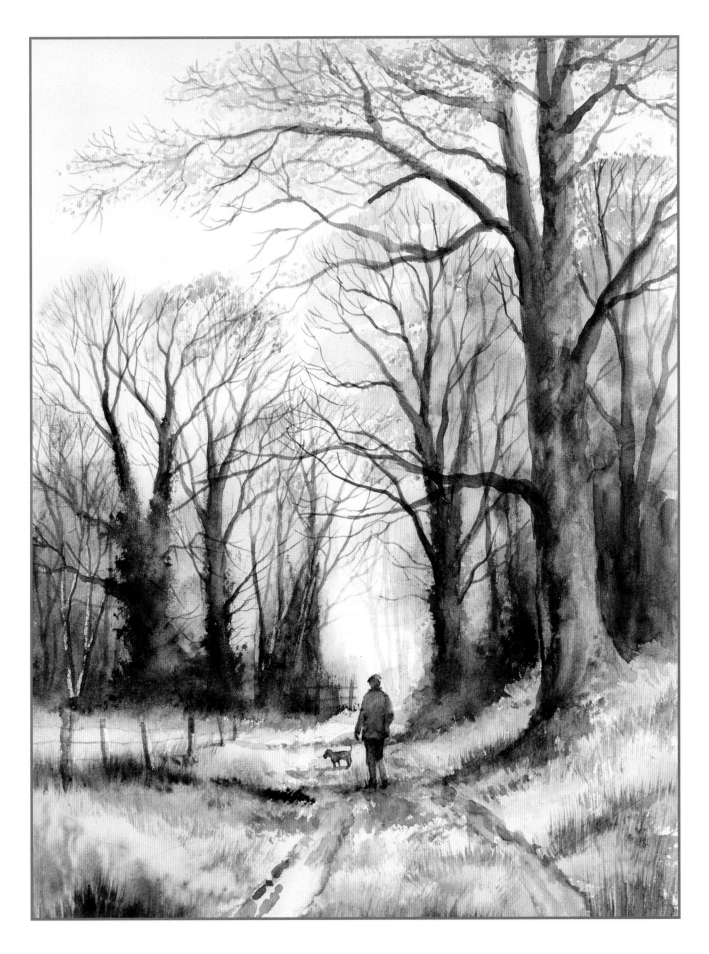

82 PAINTING A WINTER TREE

The shape of the tree was stippled with the foliage brush and a light grey mixed from ultramarine and burnt umber. Then the trunk and branches were painted into the shape with the half-rigger and a stronger mix of the same colours.

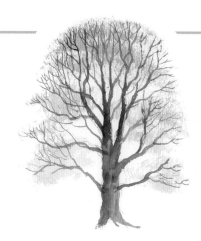

83 PAINTING A SUMMER OAK TREE

This was painted using my three ready-made greens: sunlit green was used on the lighter side, then a mix of country olive and midnight green for the shady side, leaving some gaps. The branches and the trunk were added in the same dark green mix, with the branches going through the gaps in the foliage.

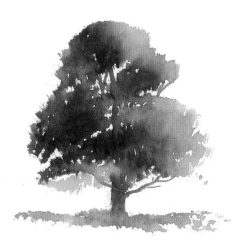

84 PAINTING AUTUMN TREES

I have used a selection of earth colours to create the autumn tones, starting with raw sienna for the lighter parts, then burnt sienna for the shaded halves of the trees. The trunks were painted in wet on dry with a dark mix of ultramarine and burnt umber. The ivy was painted in with midnight green.

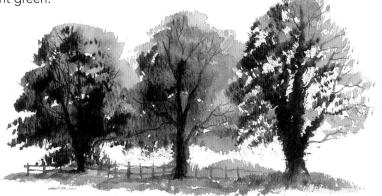

85 PAINTING A CONIFER

This was painted with the fan gogh brush. Load the brush with the darker colour first and paint from the outside in to the centre. Then load with the lighter colour and paint the other side, again from the outside in. The tree is wider at the base and gradually tapers to a point at the top.

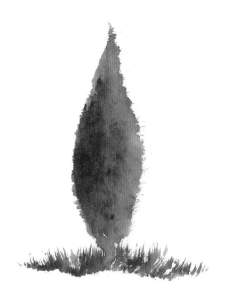

86 A FAN GOGH WEEPING WILLOW

The trunk was painted first, then the foliage was painted with the fan gogh brush. The key is not to have the brush overloaded or too wet, as this will result in a solid wash. Use the very tip of the brush to achieve a streaked effect.

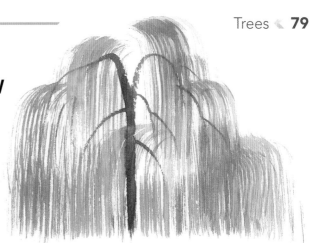

87 PAINTING AN IVY-COVERED TREE

I used the fan stippler brush with midnight green to stipple the ivy which creates the shape of the tree trunk. The shape of the tree was stippled with the fan stippler using a light mix of ultramarine and burnt umber, then the trunk and branches were painted into the shape, using the half-rigger and a stronger mix of the same colours.

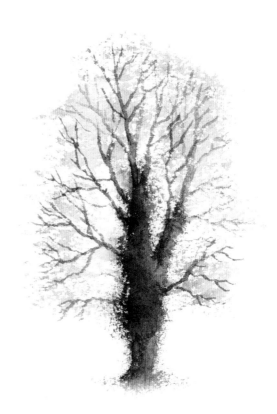

88 PAINTING BLOSSOM

The blossom effect on the tree shown bottom left was created using masking fluid. For this example I used a small brush and dotted each blossom over the shape of the tree. When dry, I painted the green foliage over the top. When the paint was dry, I removed the masking fluid to reveal the white of the paper. I then painted a pale mix of permanent rose on to some of the blossoms.

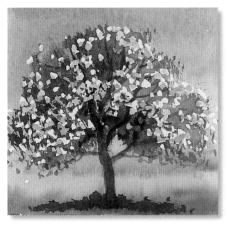
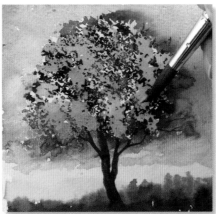

The blossom on the tree on the left was created using masking fluid applied with a sponge. I then rubbed off the masking fluid and applied a wash of permanent rose to the white parts.

89 AVOIDING BROWN FOR TREE TRUNKS

One of the most common mistakes when painting trees is painting the trunks brown. They are often either green, silver or grey but rarely brown. Note how the trunk on the right looks much more natural than the brown one on the left.

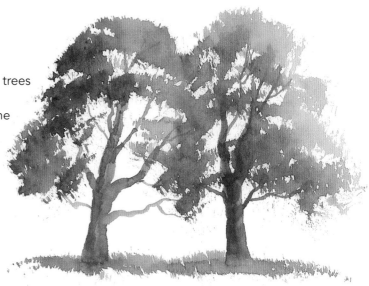

90 CREATING A PLASTIC CARD TREE TRUNK

This technique uses the surface of Rough or Not watercolour paper to create texture.

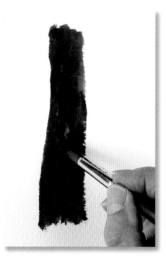 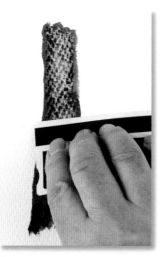 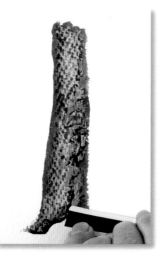 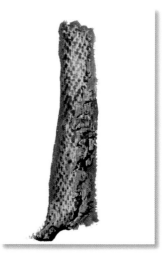

1 Use the large detail brush to paint the trunk with a thick mix of burnt umber with country olive.

2 Hold a plastic card at forty-five degrees to the paper surface and drag it down the trunk, placing more pressure on the left. This scrapes off the top layer of colour and reveals the paper texture.

3 Add more texture to the trunk using the corner of the card.

The completed trunk.

91 CREATING A SILVER BIRCH TRUNK USING A PLASTIC CARD

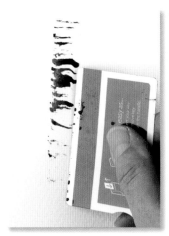 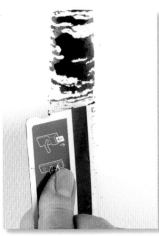 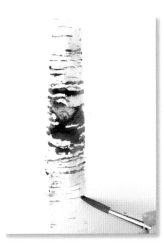

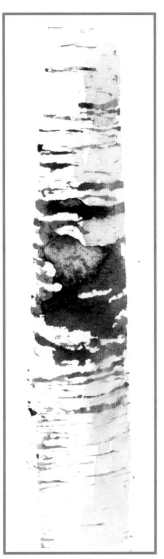

1 Make a thick mix of ultramarine and burnt umber and pick it up on the edge of a plastic card. Drag this across the paper to create the textured lines of the bark.

2 Reload the card with paint and continue. Allow to dry.

3 Use the medium detail brush and a wash of cobalt blue to paint shade on the right-hand side of the birch's trunk.

92 DRY BRUSHWORK TREE TRUNKS

This simple effect is created by dragging a round brush loaded with colour but with little water over the surface of Rough paper. The paint catches the raised part of the surface and leaves white paper in the troughs.

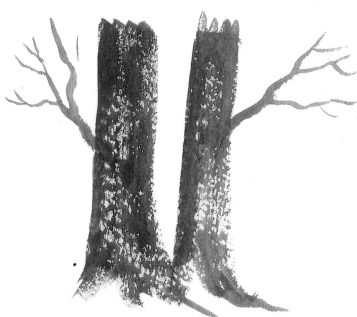

93 PAINTING PALM TREES

The trunk of the palm tree on the right was painted with a large detail brush, using the dry brush technique. The fronds were painted with the fan gogh brush in midnight green. The step-by-step sequence below shows another way of painting palm leaves.

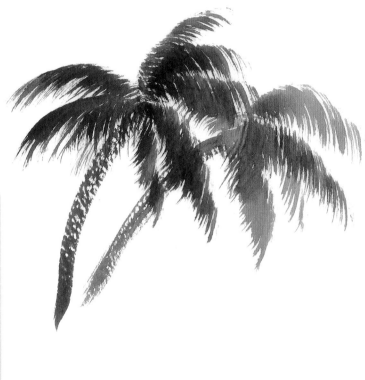

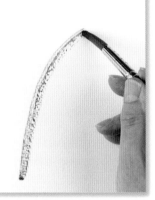 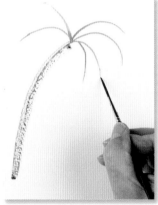

1 Paint the trunk with the large detail brush and burnt umber, using the dry brush technique.

2 Use the half-rigger with country olive to paint the spines of the palm leaves.

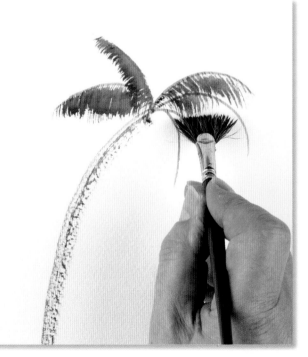

3 Use the fan gogh and country olive to paint the fronds curving down from the spines.

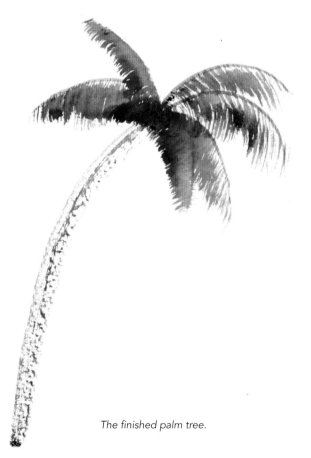

The finished palm tree.

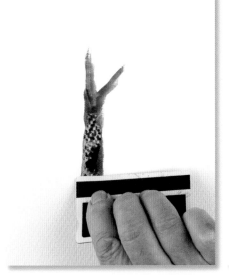 94 PAINTING A SUMMER TREE WITH FOLIAGE

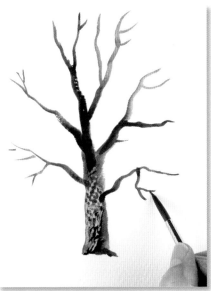

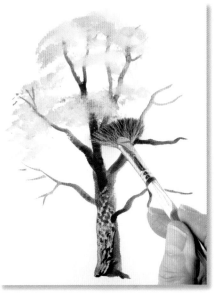

1 Paint the trunk with the large detail brush and a thick mix of burnt umber and ultramarine. Scrape the edge of a plastic card down the left-hand side to create texture. This suggests light coming from the left.

2 Add country olive to the same mix then continue painting the branches.

3 Use the fan stippler to stipple on sunlit green for the lit left-hand part of the tree. Paint over the trunk and branches.

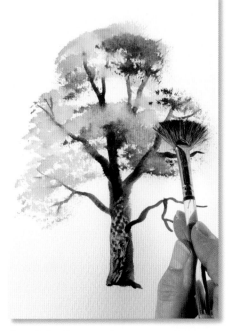

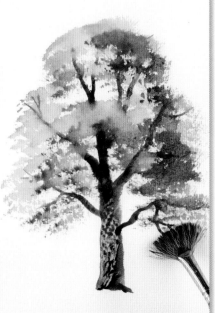

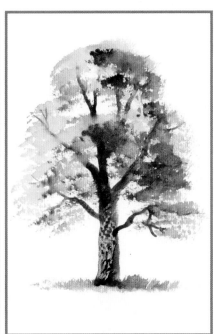

4 While this is still wet, stipple country olive over the top in the darker, shaded parts of the foliage.

5 Stipple on midnight green for the darkest parts of the foliage on the right and underneath.

The finished tree.

Grasses

When painting grasses, always paint in the direction in which the grass grows: starting from the ground and moving upwards.

95 SCRAPING OUT GRASSES WITH A BRUSH HANDLE

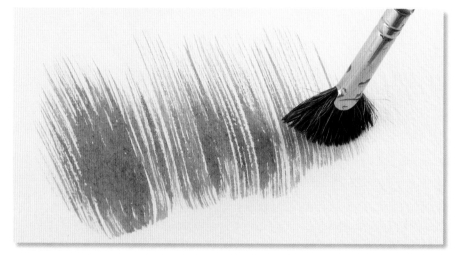

1 Flick up grasses using the fan gogh brush and a fairly thick mix.

2 Use a clear acrylic resin brush handle to scrape out more grasses from the damp paint. This handle is specially designed for scraping out.

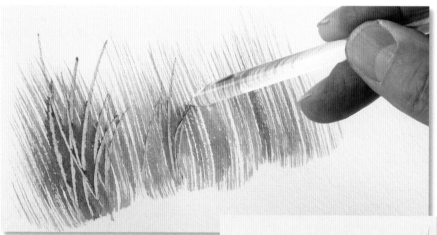

3 When the paint is dry, you can add darker grasses with a half-rigger brush to complete the effect.

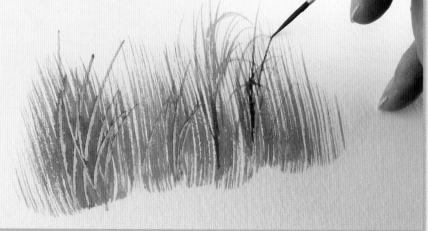

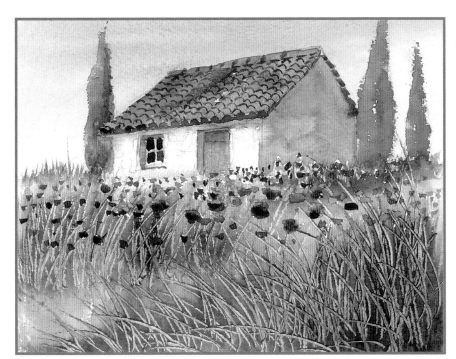

Here I painted the area first, then scraped out texture using the end of the clear acrylic resin (or px) brush.

96 PAINTING GRASSES USING MASKING FLUID AND RULING PEN

Apply masking fluid to the paper using a ruling pen. Then paint on a dark colour, making sure your brushstrokes go in the same direction as the masked-out grasses. When the paint is dry, remove the masking fluid and wash a pale colour over the white of the exposed paper.

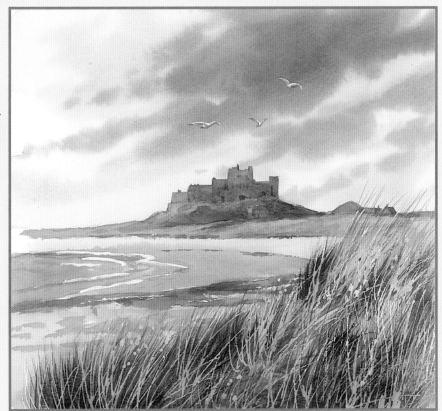

Flowers

Flowers look best painted freshly onto a white background. This is why masking fluid is often used when painting flowers.

97 PAINTING WET INTO WET POPPIES

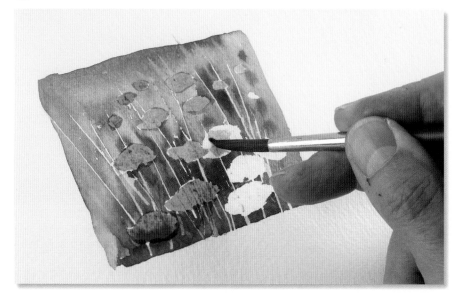

1 Remove the masking fluid ready to paint the poppies. Drop in a fairly pale mix of cadmium red.

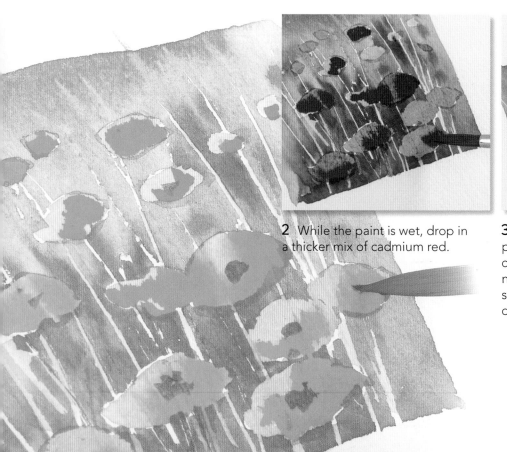

2 While the paint is wet, drop in a thicker mix of cadmium red.

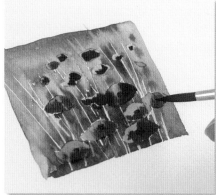

3 Allow the poppies to dry and paint in the centres using shadow colour, such as a purplish grey. Do not paint centres in all the poppies since some will be facing in a different direction.

98 PAINTING COW PARSLEY USING MASKING FLUID

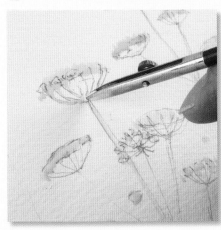

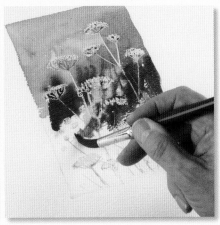

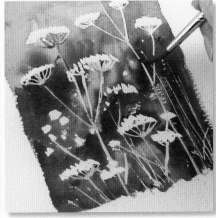

1 Apply masking fluid using a brush for the flowers and a ruling pen for the stalks.

2 Paint a blue sky and various greens wet into wet for grasses.

3 Remove the masking fluid, then paint the stems with a thin mix of sunlit green.

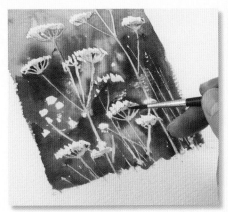

4 Add shade to the white flowers using a very thin mix of raw sienna and cobalt blue and the small detail brush.

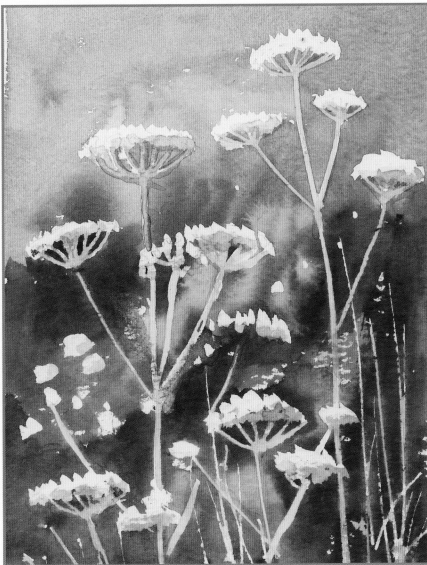

The finished painting.

⬢99 PAINTING RHODODENDRONS

The flower heads were stippled first with the foliage brush and permanent rose, then some cobalt blue was stippled on to the underside of the blooms to create the shade. The flowers in the pot were masked off with masking fluid and the colour was dropped in to each individual flower head.

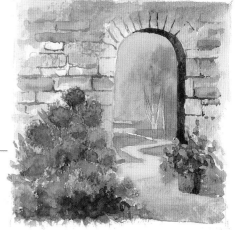

⬢100 PAINTING DAISIES

Daisies need to be drawn and masked off with care. Mask off the daisies and some grasses first, and then paint a green background wash. When that is dry, add some strong, dark brushstrokes to represent grass. When dry, remove the masking fluid. Use cadmium yellow with a hint of cadmium red for the centres of the daisies. Use burnt umber for the shaded edges of the centres. Shade the petals with a very pale wash of cobalt blue. Wash a pale green into the white of the grasses and stems.

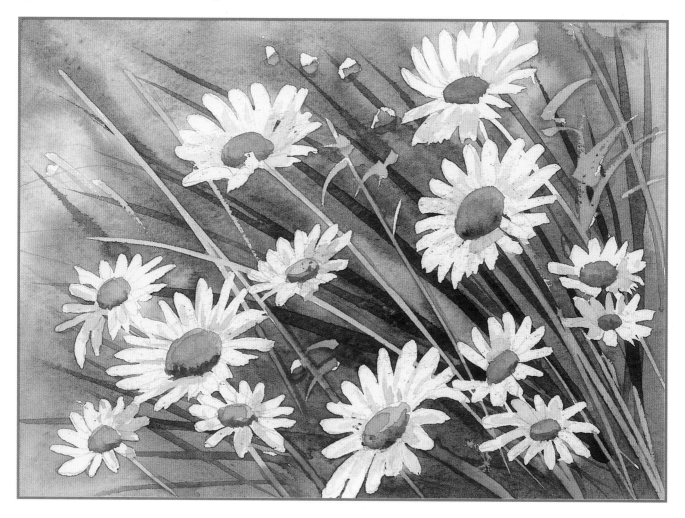

101 PAINTING BLUEBELLS

The colour mix I use for painting bluebells is simply cobalt blue and permanent rose. By varying this mix, you have a whole variety of tones and shades to create a bluebell wood.

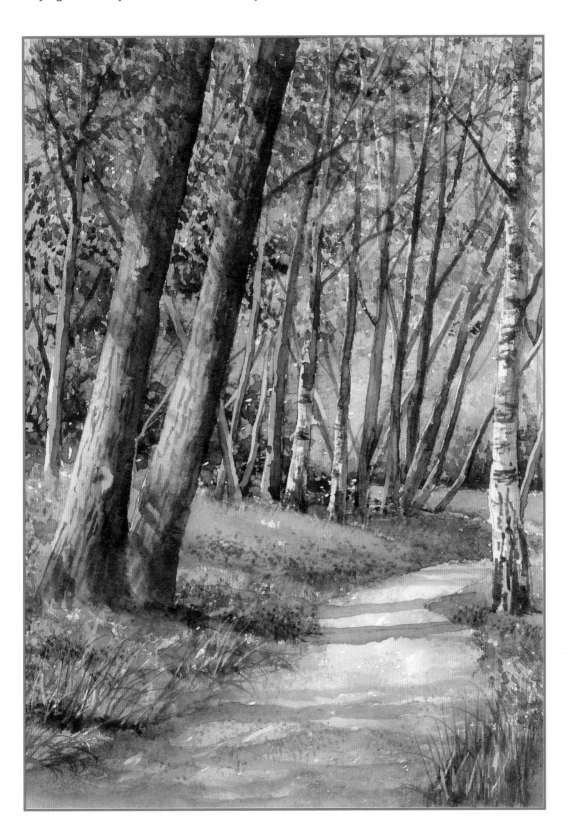

🌸 102 PAINTING FINGERPRINT POPPIES

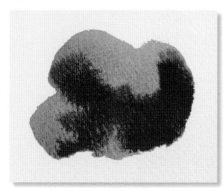 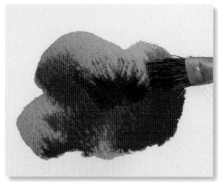 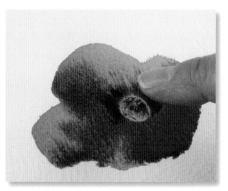

1 Paint the poppy shape with a thinner and then a thicker mix of cadmium red as before.

2 Brush in a feathered centre using shadow colour wet into wet.

3 Use your finger to make a fingerprint in the centre.

🌸 103 PAINTING TERRACOTTA POTS

Terracotta pots will often crop up in paintings, and there are many different ways of painting them. Here are a few examples of colour mixes for terracotta. The same mixes can also be used for painting pan tiles for roofs (see page 111).

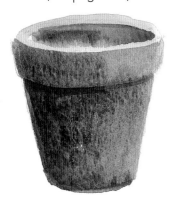 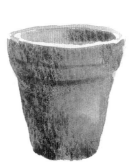 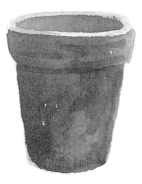

Burnt sienna and shadow　　*Burnt sienna and raw sienna*　　*Cadmium red, cadmium yellow and ultramarine*

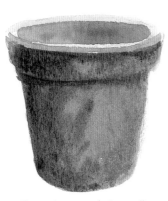 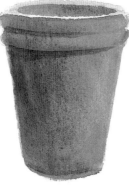 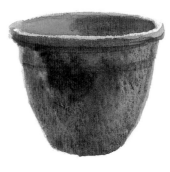

Burnt sienna, cadmium yellow and shadow with sunlit green　　*Cadmium red, raw sienna and ultramarine*　　*Burnt sienna and burnt umber with sunlit green*

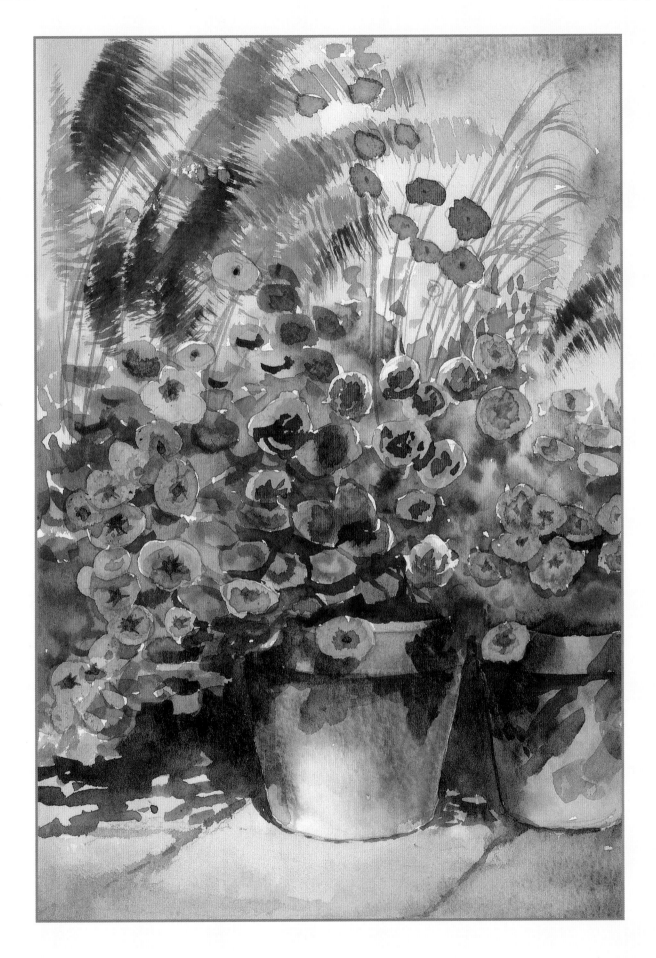

Mountains

When I paint mountains, I try not to put in too much detail as they are often just a backdrop to a painting.

❂ 104 MASKING FLUID SNOW

To preserve the white of the snow, I have used masking fluid. A dark cloud behind the mountain creates a contrast. The shade on the snow is created from a pale wash of cobalt blue.

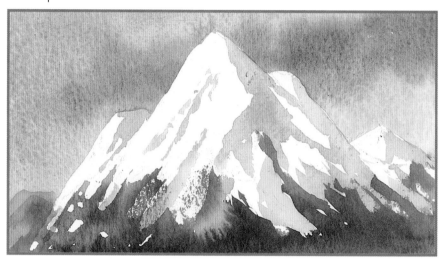

❂ 105 PAINTING MISTY MOUNTAINS

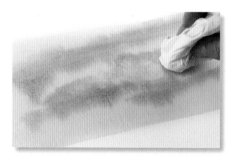

1 Paint the sky and lift out highlights in the clouds.

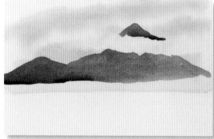

2 Paint in the mountains using ultramarine and burnt umber, leaving a space for mist as shown.

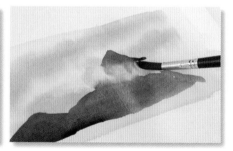

3 Allow the mountains to dry. Wet the misty area with clean water.

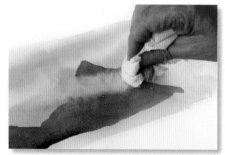

4 Lift out colour using kitchen paper.

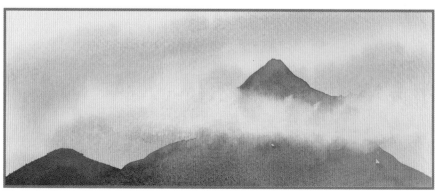

🖌 106 SCRAPING OUT MOUNTAINS WITH A PLASTIC CARD

 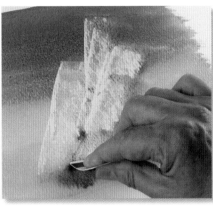 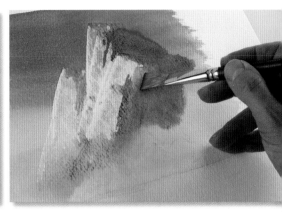

1 Paint raw sienna at the bottom, then paint ultramarine going down into the raw sienna wet into wet.

2 Take a plastic card such as an old credit card and scrape mountain shapes into the wet paint.

3 Use shadow colour and the 19mm (¾in) flat brush to darken the shaded sides of the mountains.

🖌 107 DROPPING IN RAW SIENNA

Raw sienna has a tendency to repel other colours when mixed wet into wet. This can create a useful effect.

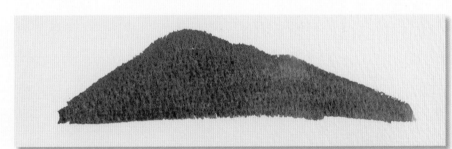

1 Paint the mountain shape using a mix of shadow colour and burnt umber.

2 While the paint is still wet, drop in raw sienna to one side. The raw sienna pushes away the darker paint to create the effect of sunlit rock.

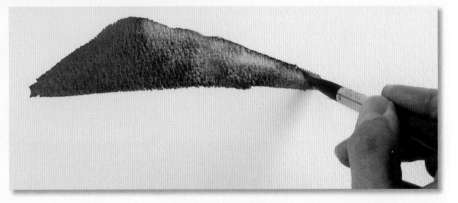

Water

Painting water is one of the biggest challenges for any artist. Water has many moods and many different forms, such as rivers, seas, ponds and dramatic waterfalls.

108 PAINTING A WATERFALL

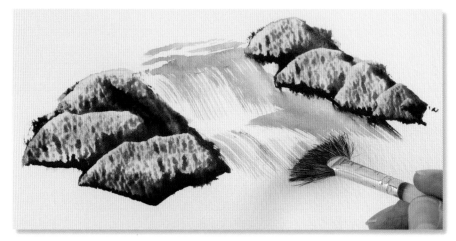

1 Paint the rocks first, then pick up cobalt blue mixed with midnight green on the fan gogh brush. Paint ripples at the top of the waterfall and then drag the brush down the path of the water.

2 Allow the paint to dry, then mix cobalt blue with ultramarine and burnt umber and darken the water's edge beneath the right-hand rocks.

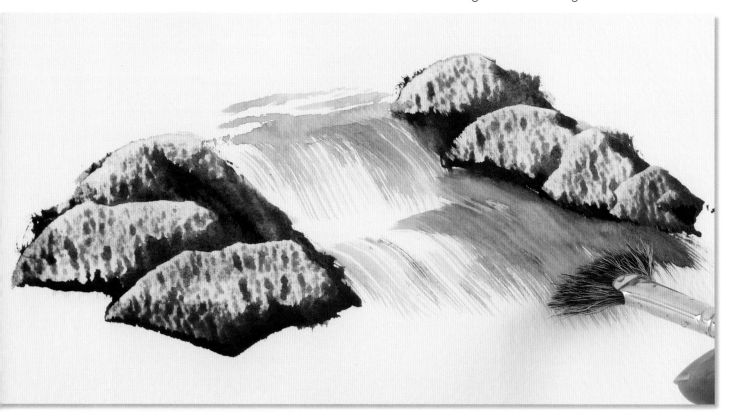

109   CREATING A MASKING FLUID WATERFALL

Carefully plan and draw the flow of the river. Mask off the foamy white water with masking fluid, painting in the direction in which the water flows. Paint the rocks in a dark colour for contrast. Use cobalt blue with a touch of midnight green to paint in the mid-tone of the water. Remove the masking fluid and refine the detail of the water with the same mix.

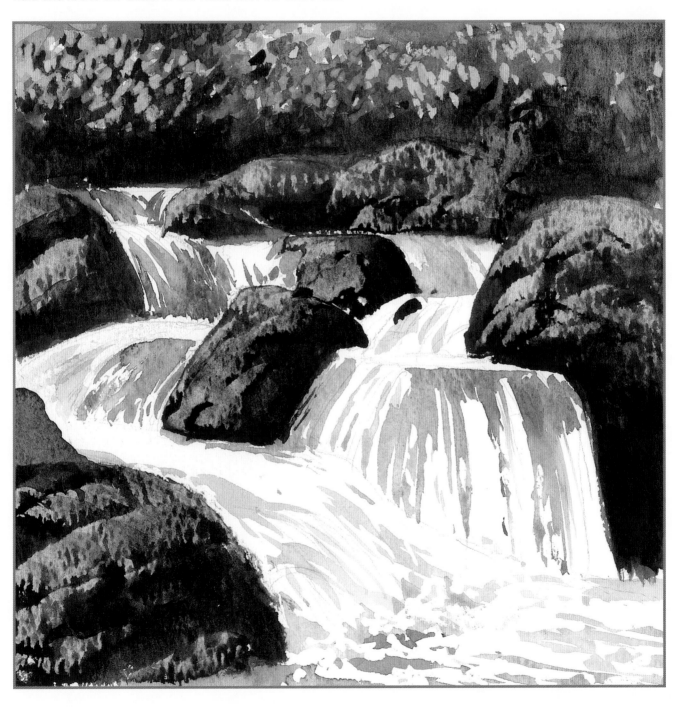

110 MASKING FLUID RIPPLES

Masking fluid is used to capture the sunlight on the water. The ripples in the far distance are painted in first with small horizontal brushstrokes. These become broader and larger as they reach the foreground.

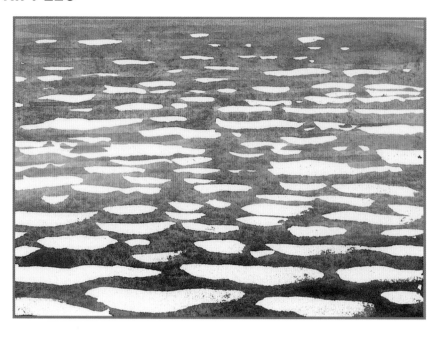

111 LIFTING OUT RIPPLES

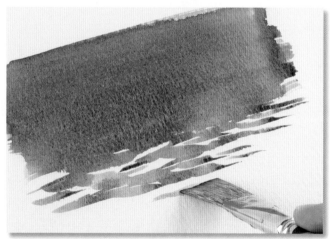

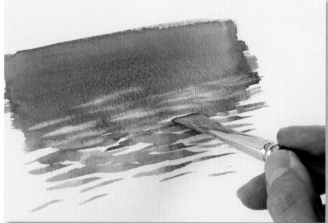

1 Take the 19mm (¾in) flat brush and paint a flat wash for the water. Towards the bottom, move the brush from side to side to create a rippled effect.

2 Before the paint dries, wash the brush, squeeze out the excess water and lift out ripples from the wet wash.

112 DRAGGING DOWN REFLECTIONS

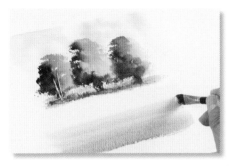 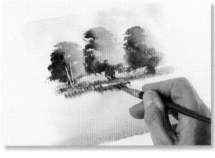 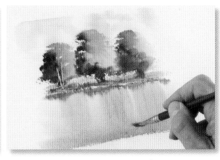

1 Wet the water area with clean water and the wizard brush. Paint a thin wash of ultramarine from the bottom. The water on the paper means that the wash will fade towards the top.

2 Paint reflections of the bank colours and drag them down slightly into the water, working wet into wet.

3 Pick up the lighter tree colours and drag them down into the water as before, wet into wet.

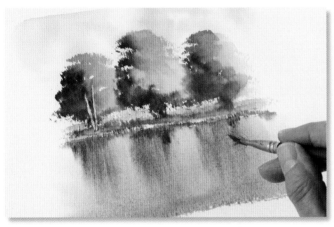 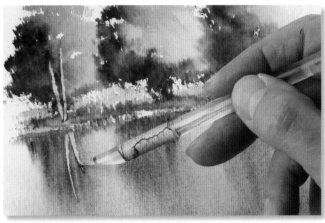

4 While the paint is still wet, drag some darker greens down into the water to reflect the trees and other details above.

5 Use the handle end of a px brush to scrape out the reflection of the left-hand tree trunk.

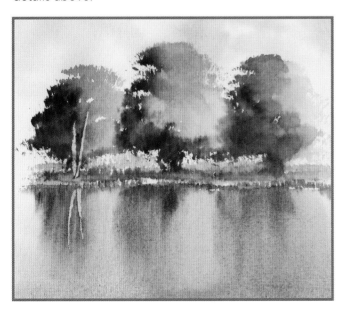

The finished scene.

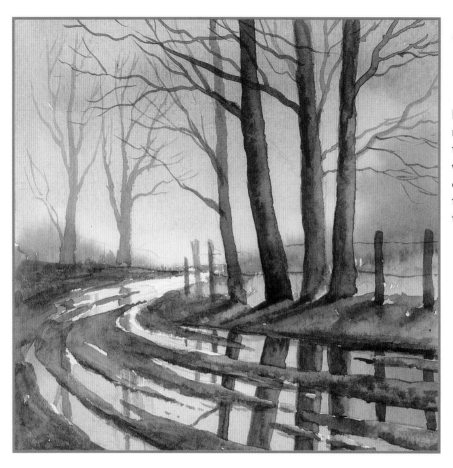

113 REFLECTIONS OF POSTS AND TREES

If you are painting puddles in a road, always paint reflections in them. This tells the viewer that it is water. Be sure to observe the scene or reference photograph carefully so that you get the angles of posts and trees right.

114 BREAKING WAVES

I have relied heavily on using masking fluid for the white foam in this painting. The movement of the wave hitting the rock is exaggerated by flicking up the masking fluid to represent spray. This adds drama to a painting.

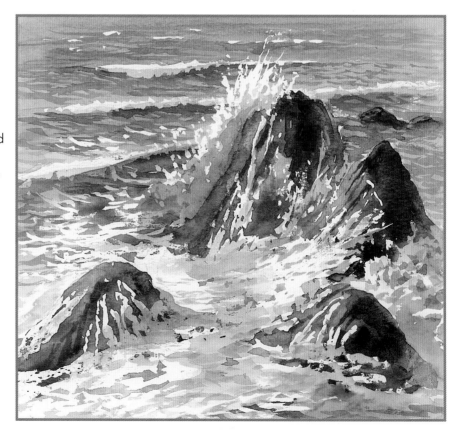

115 PAINTING CHOPPY WATER

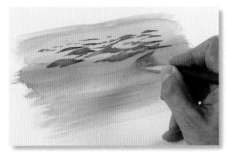

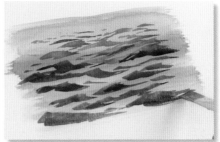

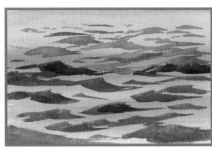

1 Paint a background with a wash of ultramarine and let it dry. Use the 19mm (¾in) flat brush to paint diagonal strokes with a stronger mix of ultramarine.

2 As you come towards the foreground, use a strong mix of ultramarine and midnight green and make bigger marks.

The finished painting.

116 USING MASKING TAPE TO PAINT A STRAIGHT HORIZON

Before using masking tape, rub the sticky side with your fingers or apply it first to your clothes. This makes it less tacky and less likely to pull off paint when removed.

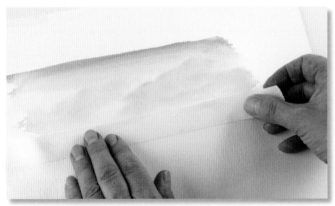

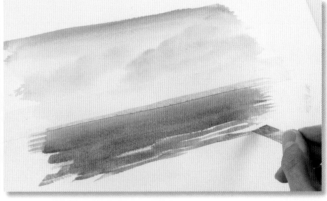

1 Paint the sky first, let it dry and then apply masking tape in a straight line at the bottom, with the bottom of the tape where you want the horizon to be.

2 Use the 19mm (¾in) flat brush to paint the sea, going over the bottom of the masking tape.

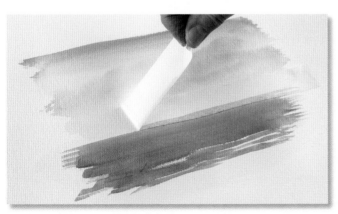

3 When the paint is dry, peel off the masking tape, making sure you pull it upwards, away from the horizon line.

117 USING A SPONGE TO LIFT OUT SPRAY

The tip for this technique is speed. As soon as the paint is applied, the spray is lifted off the paper with a damp sponge. When the painting is dry, the detail is added.

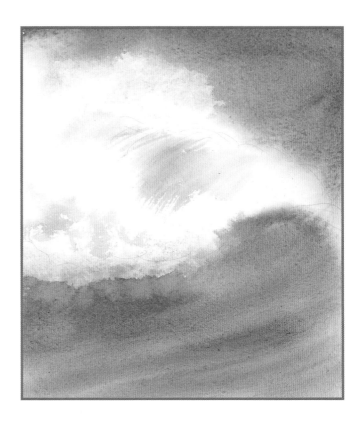

118 MASKING FLUID SPRAY

This was done by applying masking fluid with a natural sponge. You can also use screwed-up kitchen paper. The shade on the spray was painted in with cobalt blue and a touch of permanent rose.

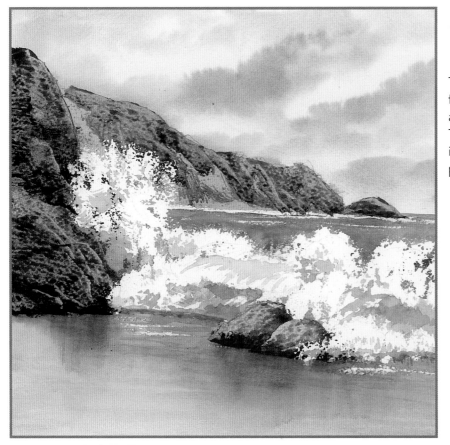

119 REFLECTIONS IN SHALLOW WATER

Mask off the surf lines first, and paint the sky. Paint the cliff using the rock painting techniques shown on page 104, then wet the whole sea area. Drag the cliff colours vertically down to create reflections on the beach, then merge them into blue on the left-hand side to reflect the sky. Remove the masking fluid and touch in a light blue for the detail on the surf lines.

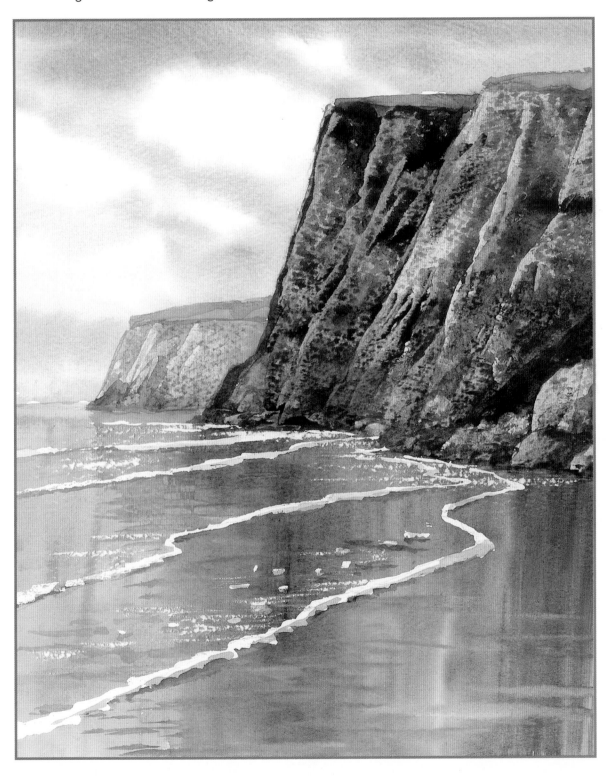

Beaches

A lot of emphasis is placed on painting water, but the shoreline and beaches are often neglected. Here are a few tips on how to tackle these foregrounds.

120 SPATTERING PEBBLES WITH MASKING FLUID

To apply the masking fluid I used a stiff-haired toothbrush. Then some larger pebbles were dotted in with masking fluid applied with a small round brush. When the masking fluid was dry, I painted in the background colour. When dry, I removed the masking fluid and washed a light colour over the stones. I finished off with some shade underneath the larger stones.

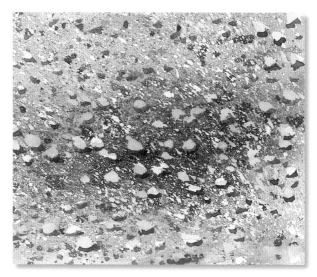

121 STIPPLING PEBBLES

The background colour was washed in with raw sienna, then with a stronger mix of raw sienna, and the pebbles were stippled using the foliage brush. Finally some shade was added to the undersides of the pebbles in the foreground to create form.

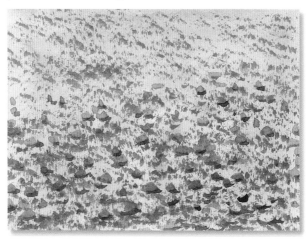

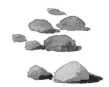

122 PAINTING SAND

The colour I have used for the sand is mostly raw sienna. I have added some shadow colour in amongst the sand dunes for shade.

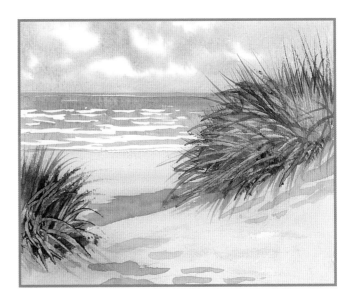

123 A MASKING FLUID SURF LINE

You can paint in surf lines and ripples with masking fluid. Paint the beach in with raw sienna, then wash the blue down into the raw sienna while it is still wet. Remove the masking fluid, then paint in the darker detail underneath the surf lines and the darker ripples.

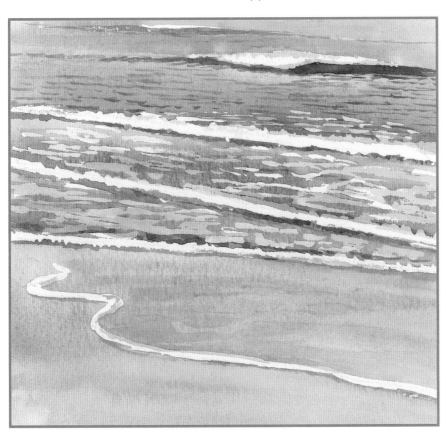

Rocks

Rocks have varied surfaces and colours: warm sandstone contrasts with hard, cool granite, so your choice of colours is as important as creating texture.

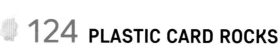

124 PLASTIC CARD ROCKS

The surface of the paper will create the textured effect so choosing the right paper is important. Choose Rough paper for this technique.

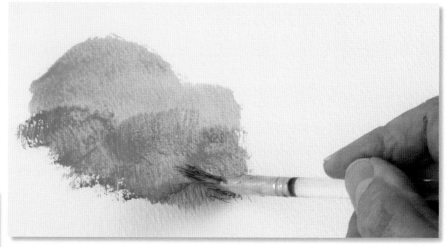

1 Take a stiff-haired brush such as the fan stippler and apply the lightest colour, raw sienna, first. The mix should be very thick. Add country green for moss.

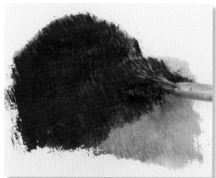

2 Paint thick ultramarine and burnt umber on top.

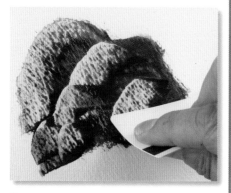

3 Scrape an old credit card or other plastic card over the surface to remove paint to create rock shapes. Start with the furthest rocks and come forwards.

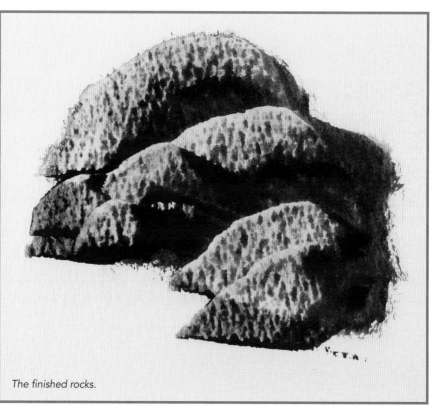

The finished rocks.

125 FOLIAGE BRUSH ROCKS

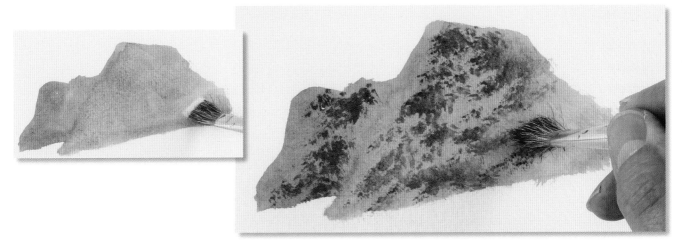

1 Paint on a thick mix of raw sienna with a little ultramarine, then stipple on texture using the foliage brush and burnt umber mixed with ultramarine.

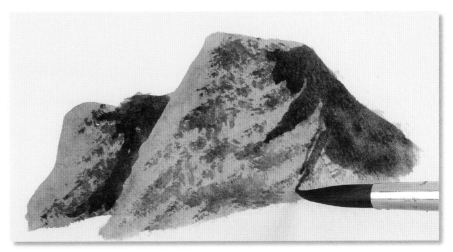

2 Use a round brush to paint on a darker shade of the same mix to create shadows.

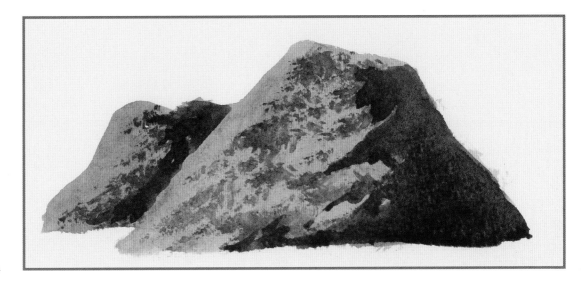

The finished rocks.

Cliffs

Whatever cliff you are painting, whether chalk or hard stone, the choices remain the same, those of colour and texture.

126 PAINTING WHITE CLIFFS

The technique used here is the dry brush method, dragging the almost dry brush lightly over the surface of the paper, leaving the paint on the raised part of the paper and the white remaining in the dips.

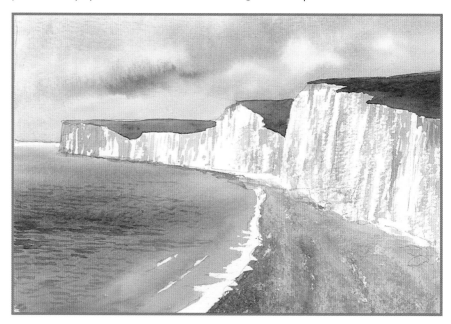

127 CLING FILM CLIFFS

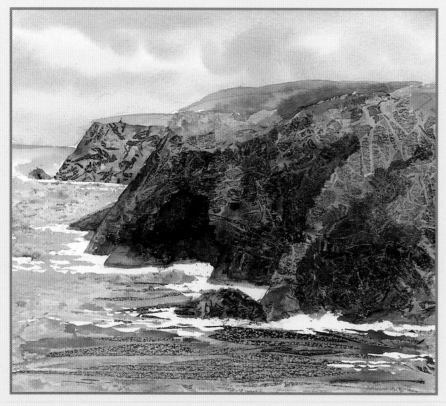

This is a relatively simple way to create texture using cling film. Mix plenty of colour, in this case ultramarine and burnt umber, then paint it on to the surface of the cliff face. While it is still wet, scrunch up cling film and press it on to the surface of the painting. Allow this to dry naturally. Once dry, remove the cling film to reveal a beautiful, natural-looking texture.

🌀 128 PLASTIC CARD CLIFFS

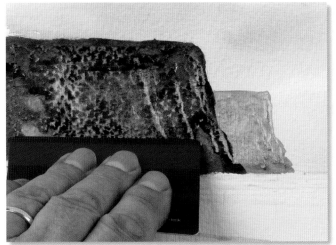

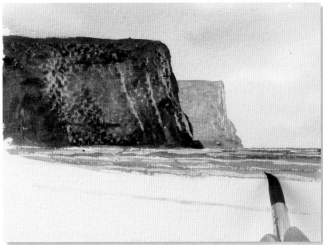

1 Draw the scene and mask the surf with a brush and masking fluid. Use the wizard to wet the sky area, then paint it with raw sienna. Paint in clouds with ultramarine, wet into wet. Allow to dry. Paint the distant cliff with the large detail brush and a pale mix of ultramarine and burnt umber, then use a plastic card to scrape out texture. Paint the nearer cliff with a stronger mix, then scrape out texture with a card in the same way.

2 Use a mix of ultramarine and midnight green and a side-to-side motion of the brush to paint the sea.

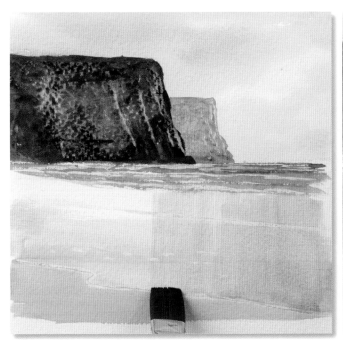

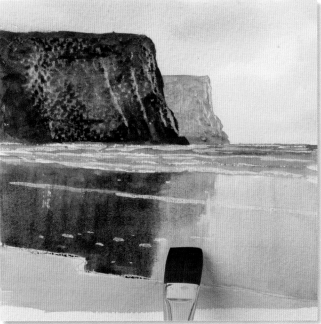

3 Paint the beach with raw sienna and a little burnt sienna. Wet the area between this and the sea and use the 19mm (¾in) flat brush to stroke down a pale mix of ultramarine to suggest wet sand.

4 Stroke down a strong mix of ultramarine and burnt umber below the cliff, and a paler mix below the more distant cliff to create reflections in the wet sand. Allow to dry and remove the masking fluid.

Boats

It is a shame that timid artists shy away from painting boats, as they can add something special to a scene.

129 DRAWING BOATS

Remember to draw what you see, not what you think you see. The shape of the boat is curved, so we tend to draw all the lines with a curve, but all is not what you think – look out for the straight lines.

Looking at the boat drawings below, you might think at first that the shapes are all made up of curved lines. However, if you hold a straight edge against the drawings, you can see that the back line of both is in fact straight.

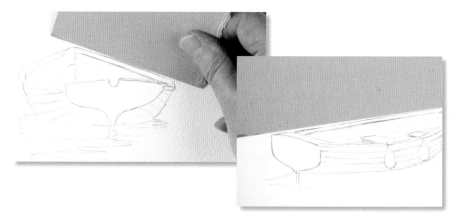

In the same way the boat in the painting below looks like a curved shape within the scene, but holding a straight edge against it shows once again that the back line is straight.

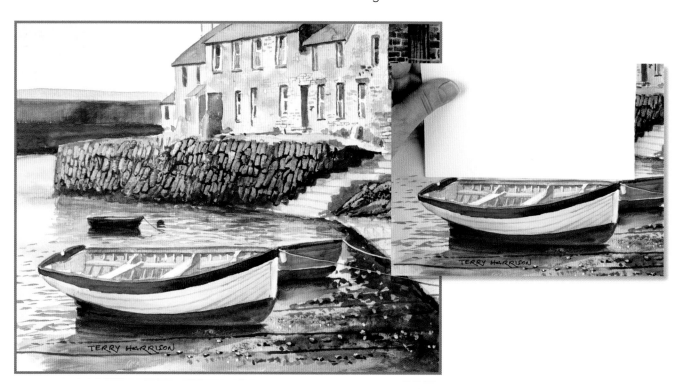

130 BOATS WITH CHARACTER

Choose something with character; avoid plastic boats. If the boat you wish to paint is plastic, why not change it into something more rustic?

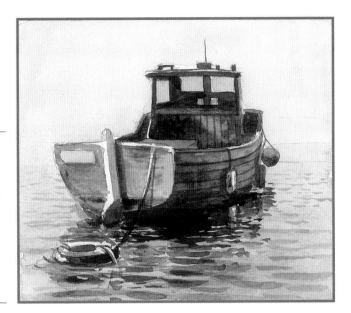

131 PAINTING THE WATERLINE

Use dark colours along the waterline. This gives the impression that the boat is sitting in water rather than on it.

132 CONCEAL THE INSIDE

Make sure you do not reveal too much of the inside of the boat, or this will give the impression that the boat is tilting forwards.

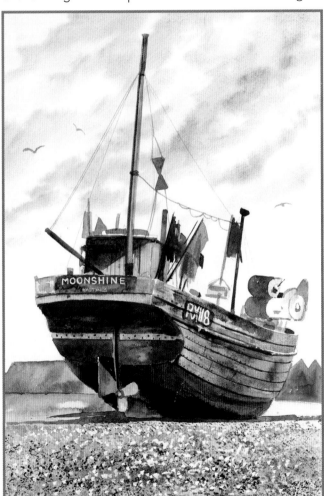

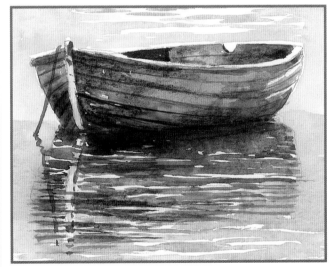

Roofs

Painting roofs can get quite technical. There is a whole variety of materials used for roofing, so time should be spent establishing what material the roof is made of. Roofs can be tackled in so many different ways.

133 HOW TO FIND THE CORRECT PITCH OF ANY ROOF

Begin by drawing a rectangle, which is the front of the building. If you join each corner diagonally (making a cross), the centre of the cross is the centre of the building. Draw a vertical line through the centre of the cross to the top of the roof (the height will obviously vary). Whatever height you choose to make the roof, you join the top two corners of the building to create the apex of the roof. This sounds complicated, but once you have a go, it all makes complete sense.

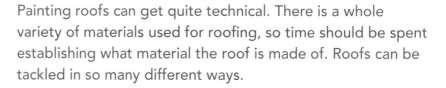

134 A SLATE ROOF

The most distinctive thing about a slate roof is the colour. Depending on the lighting conditions the roof can appear warm or cool but it will always be grey. In this example I have used a combination of raw umber with raw sienna and some green dropped into the paint when it was still wet.

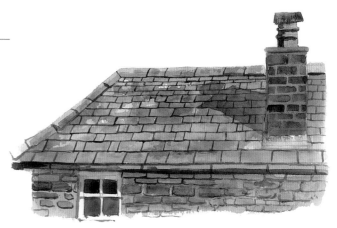

135 A THATCHED ROOF

The most common mistake is to paint a thatched roof brown or yellow. If you take the time to look at a thatched roof, you will see that the colour is often grey. I have used shadow, ultramarine and raw sienna. The texture was achieved by applying the paint with the wizard brush.

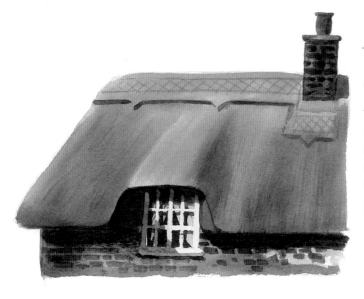

136 A CLAY TILED ROOF

The tiles on this roof are plain, flat clay tiles. The basic colour is burnt sienna with other colours dropped in to achieve a mottled effect. The characteristic of these tiles is that they can be uneven, so the horizontal lines are painted with a half-rigger and uneven, wavy lines.

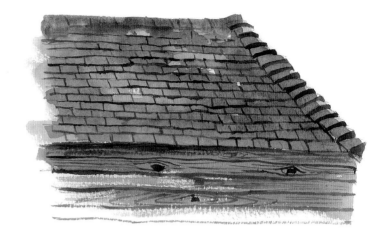

137 A TIN ROOF

When painting corrugated tin roofs, it is important to give the impression of uniform corrugation. Do not paint this too loosely: the detailed lines must be evenly spaced and the edge of the tin panels will have a wavy, uneven edge.

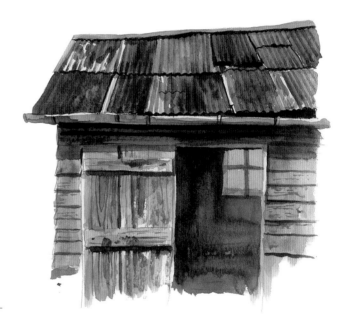

138 PAN TILES

There are two things to consider: colour and the distinctive pattern. The colours are bright and varied (see the mixes for terracotta pots on page 90). The vertical tile ridges are evenly spaced and each tile is painted with a semicircle, narrowing towards the top of the roof. Tiles in the gully are reversed like a smile shape.

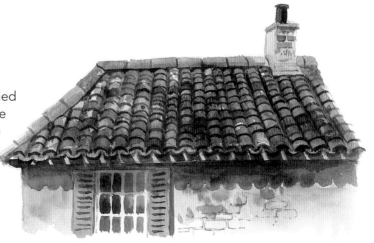

Walls

Materials used in building houses are many and varied. Painting them is mostly about suggesting textures: for example those of flints, stone or plaster.

139 SCRAPING OUT TO CREATE DRY STONE WALLS

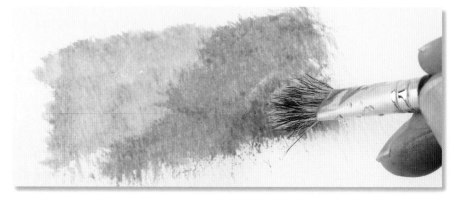

1 Use the foliage brush to paint on a thick mix of raw sienna, followed by one of sunlit green on top.

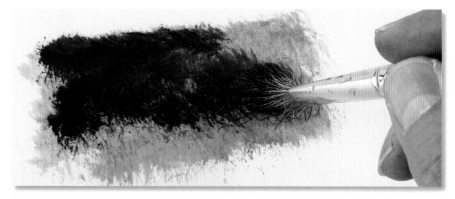

2 Make a thick mix of ultramarine and burnt umber and stipple this on top.

3 Use the end of a px (clear acrylic resin) brush handle to scrape out shapes for stones.

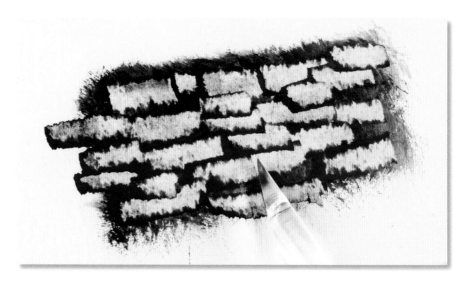

140 AN ALTERNATIVE DRY STONE WALL

Apply the lighter colours first, and then a dark brown mix on top, as before. Use the brush handle to scrape out rounder, more irregular shapes to imply stones.

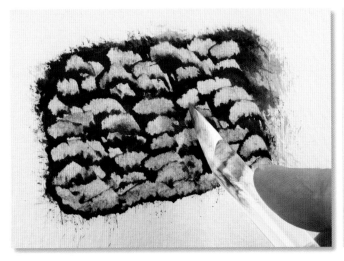

142 A FLINT WALL

Paint in a background wash and let it dry. Stipple on texture in various colours using the foliage brush. Use the half-rigger and a dark mix to pick out the shadows round stones, suggesting irregular, rounded shapes.

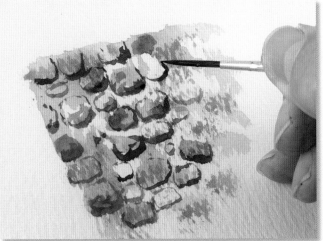

141 A RED BRICK WALL

Paint a pale background first and allow it to dry. Then use the medium detail brush to paint bricks with one stroke for each. While the paint is wet, drop in other colours for variation.

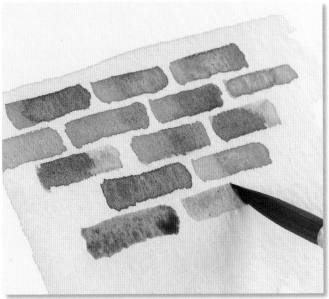

143 A RUSTIC STONE WALL

Paint the background and allow it to dry. Stipple on texture using the foliage brush, then paint in a dark shadow under each stone using the half-rigger.

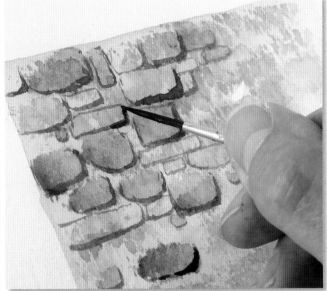

144 A DETAILED STONE WALL

The texture and detail can be enhanced by using some white gouache.

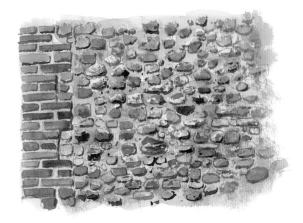

145 A DETAILED BRICK WALL

To make the bricks appear three-dimensional, paint a thin, dark shadow on the underside of each brick.

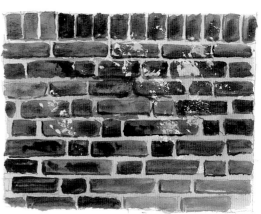

146 A RUSTIC WALL WITH PEELING PLASTER

Although this is a very rustic wall, the bricks and stones are carefully painted to avoid the vertical joints lining up. So the rules for painting a brick or stone wall are the same as for building one!

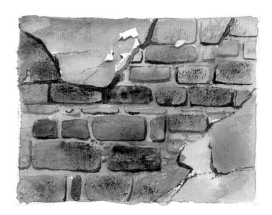

147 A PLASTERED WALL

To add texture to what would appear to be a flat surface, some of the plaster could be removed to reveal stonework underneath. A dark shadow is then placed on the underside of the plaster to give the impression that the plaster sits on top of the brick.

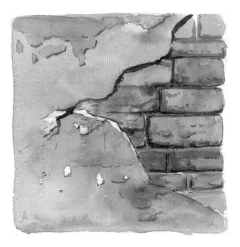

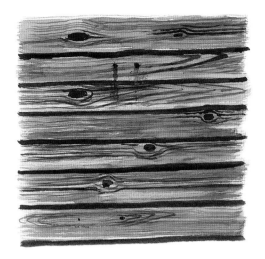

148 WEATHERBOARDS

To give the impression of the overlap, a dark line is needed, and this line could be painted with a slight wobble for a weathered look. The horizontal wood grain was painted using the wizard and the detail of the knots enhanced with a half-rigger.

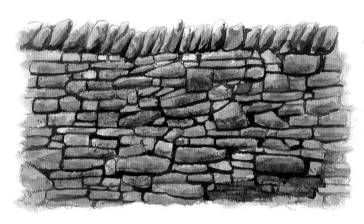

149 YORKSHIRE STONE

The dominant colour of the stonework is grey, which is a combination of burnt umber and ultramarine, but adding other colours such as burnt sienna, raw sienna and various greens creates a more mellow appearance. The detail is painted with the half-rigger.

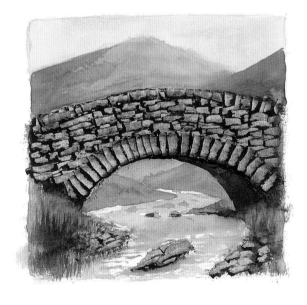

150 A BRIDGE

This technique is exactly the same as the scraping-out technique for walls described on page 112. The arch of the bridge is created by scraping vertical blocks downwards, following the curve of the arch. A shadow is then placed underneath.

Windows & doors

Whether they are clean and bright or rustic and charming, windows and doors make great studies on their own, and it pays to get them right when you are painting the whole building. If a door is open, it can invite you into a scene, just as an open gate can lead you into a landscape. Windows create opportunities for reflections and for details such as curtains and shutters.

Windows
Windows are often neglected as part of a building, but they can add so much character to a painting.

151 REFLECTIONS

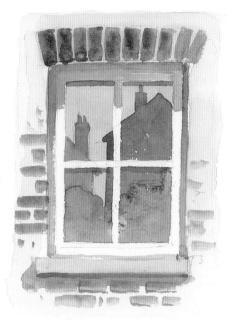

When you look at a window from the outside, you do not always see a black hole: what you see are reflections on the glass. These are often reflections of trees or buildings behind you. When you are painting a reflected building, create a simple roof and chimney silhouette and avoid any details.

152 NET CURTAINS

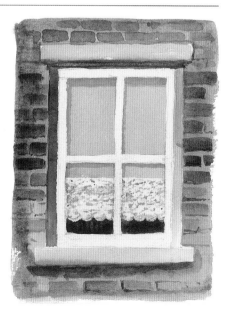

The window frames of this painting were first painted with masking fluid and some candle wax was applied to the textured part of the net curtains. Then a light grey wash was applied over the windowpanes, allowing the paint on the wax to create the texture of the net. When this was dry, the masking fluid was removed to reveal the window frame.

153 LIGHTED WINDOWS

To make a painting interesting, you could choose to paint the subject at dusk or at night. The lighted window should always be the lightest part of the painting. A good idea to create this effect is to apply a pale wash of colour over the entire picture, leaving the lighted window unpainted. Later you can add a warm yellow to the lighted area to introduce some colour. The window frames should be painted dark over a light background.

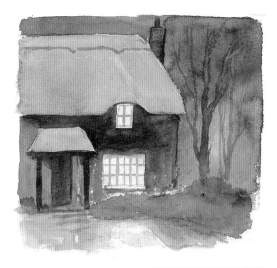

154 SHUTTERS

A great subject for a painting is a sunlit, shuttered window. An added bonus is a brightly coloured window box. In this example I used masking fluid on the window frames and also the flower heads, but look closely at the inside of the window: the folds of the curtains are carefully painted in over the masking fluid, and a deep shadow is added on the top half of the curtains. This adds depth to the painting. Do not forget to put shadows under the shutters and also the flowers.

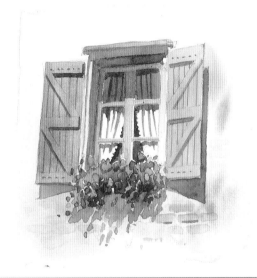

Doors

A doorway can be a fascinating subject for a painting. My favourite doorways to paint would fall into the rustic category, mostly because they are easier to paint.

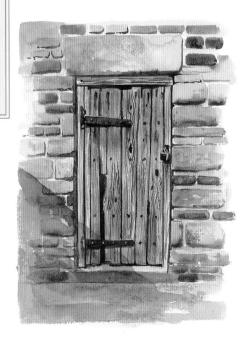

155 A RUSTIC DOOR

When you look at some doors, you can tell straight away that they are ancient. They might be an original feature of the building, and how nice it is to see these have not been replaced with a modern alternative. To make this door look weathered and old, I have made the top and bottom uneven, removed some of the wood panels to reveal the dark gap and painted the door panels with an uneven, knotted texture. Using the wizard brush creates the wood grain effect. The top hinge was painted at a slight angle with rust stains around the metalwork.

156 AN OPEN DOOR

To make this painting tell a story, I have left the door ajar. Having the door slightly open leads you into the painting and leaves the viewer wondering what lies beyond. To add extra colour and interest to the painting I have placed some flowerpots in the foreground.

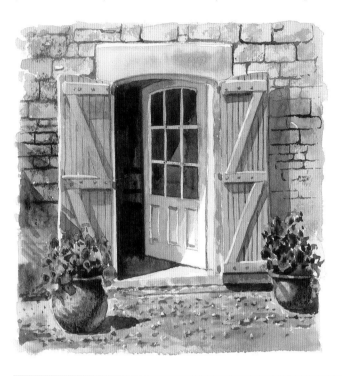

157 A PORCH

A doorway can be made more elaborate by the addition of a porch. The most common fault with painting these is not leaving enough room at the top of the door. The porch must be either the same height or taller than the door to allow someone to walk under it. Porches are very common on quaint cottages and can be enhanced with the addition of some roses round the doorway. A little bit corny, but why not?

158 USING TEXTURE PASTE TO CREATE A RUSTIC DOOR

The painting opposite was done on watercolour paper coated with acrylic texture paste and then watercolour ground as shown on page 60.

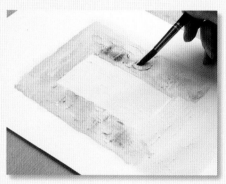

1 Paint the brickwork around the door with the large detail brush and raw sienna. While this is wet, drop in burnt sienna wet into wet.

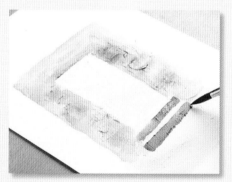

2 Still painting wet into wet, paint the shadowed parts of the brickwork and steps with shadow colour.

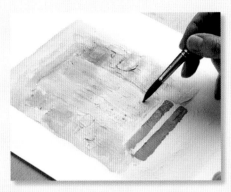

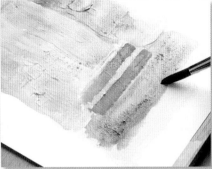

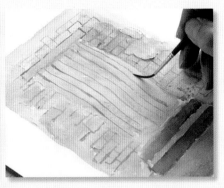

3 Paint the door with cobalt blue, then drop in raw sienna.

4 Mix a pale wash of shadow and burnt sienna and paint the lighter parts of the steps and dappled shadow in the foreground. Allow these to dry.

5 Use the half-rigger and a mix of burnt umber and ultramarine to paint the details of the brickwork and door planks.

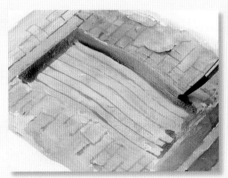

6 Change to the medium detail brush and paint the shadow in the door recess with a mix of cobalt blue and shadow.

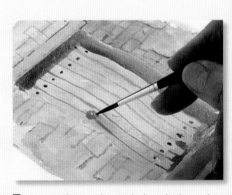

7 Paint the nails and doorknb with the small detail brush and burnt umber. Finish off by adding rust from the nails in burnt sienna.

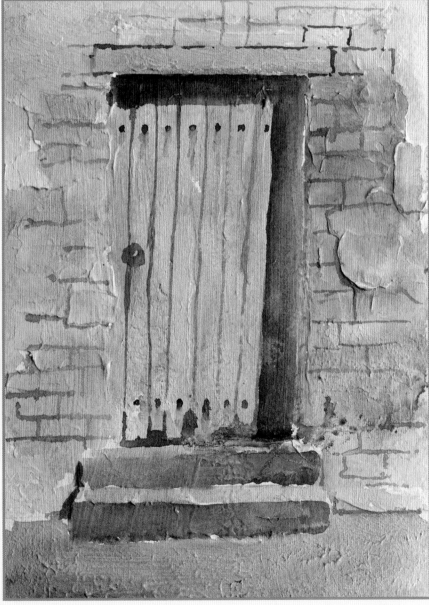

The finished door.

Stiles, gates & fences

When you are out in the countryside, you don't have to look too far to realise that humans have their part to play in the landscape. These manmade items can add pleasing details to a composition, and they often form the focal point. A stile and signpost create the illusion of a walk in the country – but don't forget to add a fence to make them credible.

159 PAINTING A STILE

One of my favourite subjects to paint is a country stile. It is not a complicated structure and there are so many different varieties to choose from. One thing to remember when painting a stile is that it is a means of climbing over a fence and the reason for the fence is to keep animals in a field, so don't forget to complete the fence!

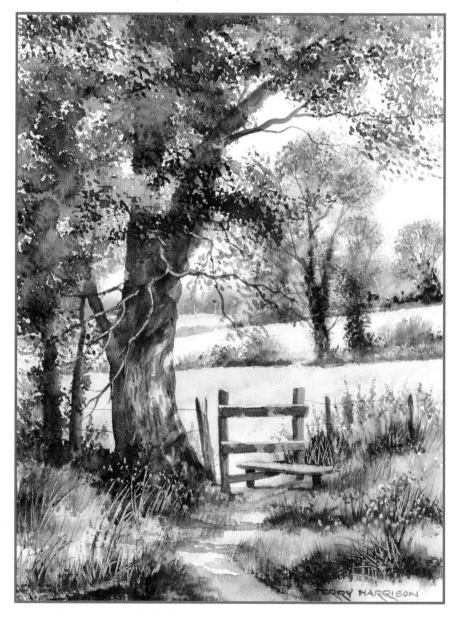

160 PAINTING A FIVE-BAR GATE

I have been told in the past that you can tell the region of the country by the style of a gate, but I think nowadays, anything goes.

The gate in this painting is what I would call a typical five-bar gate. I have used masking fluid for the left-hand side so when the painting is complete, the right-hand side is dark against light and the left-hand side is in sunlight, light against dark. Leaving the gate ajar will lead you into the painting. (You should always follow the country code and keep gates closed if that is how you find them, but open them to paint them!)

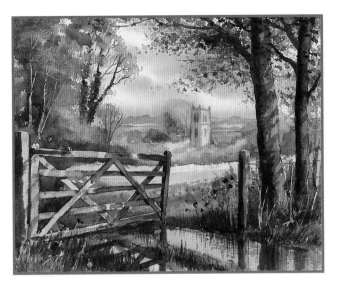

161 ADDING A FENCE AND OTHER DETAILS

A painting can be greatly improved by the addition of a fence, stile and signpost.

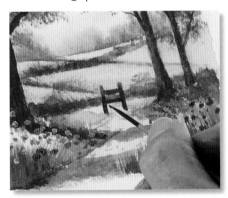

1 When the painting is dry, paint a stile using a half-rigger and a mix of country olive and burnt umber.

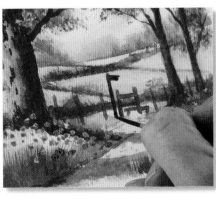

2 Paint in a fence in the same way and add a signpost.

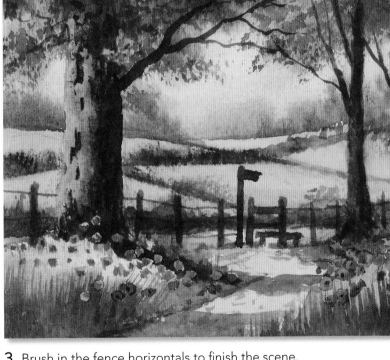

3 Brush in the fence horizontals to finish the scene.

Winter scenes

Painting snow on white paper is obviously going to create a challenge; I rely heavily on masking fluid to help me achieve the effects I want.

162 PAINTING A SNOW SCENE

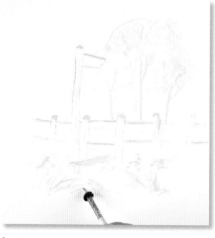

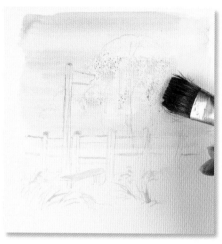

1 Draw the scene. Use kitchen paper to dab masking fluid onto the trees, then an old clogged up masking fluid brush to mask the tops of the fence, stile and signpost. Finally use a colour shaper to mask grasses in the foreground.

2 Wet the background down to the ground with the golden leaf brush, then paint on ultramarine.

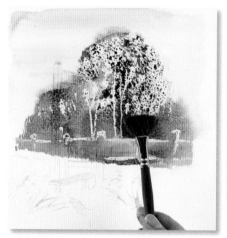

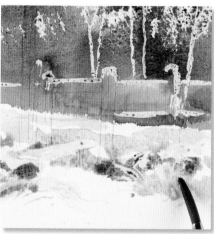

3 Use the fan gogh to paint the trees and the dark area behind the stile, then drop in raw sienna.

4 Use the medium detail brush and cobalt blue to paint snow shadows over the foreground masking fluid, then drop in burnt sienna wet into wet to suggest undergrowth. Allow to dry.

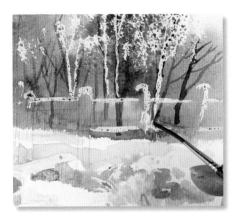

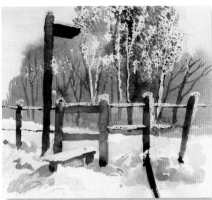

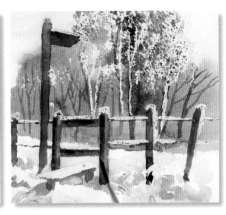

5 Change to the half-rigger and paint tree trunks among the mass of trees with a mix of ultramarine and burnt umber.

6 Paint the stile, signpost and fence with the medium detail brush and a mix of ultramarine and burnt umber. Allow to dry.

7 Use the small detail brush and a darker mix of the same colours to paint the shaded parts of the woodwork.

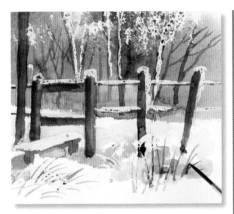

8 Paint grasses in the foreground with the half-rigger and burnt umber. Allow to dry.

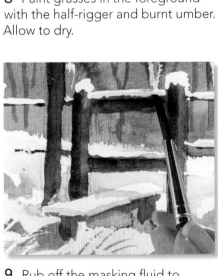

9 Rub off the masking fluid to reveal the snow, then add shadow with the small detail brush and cobalt blue.

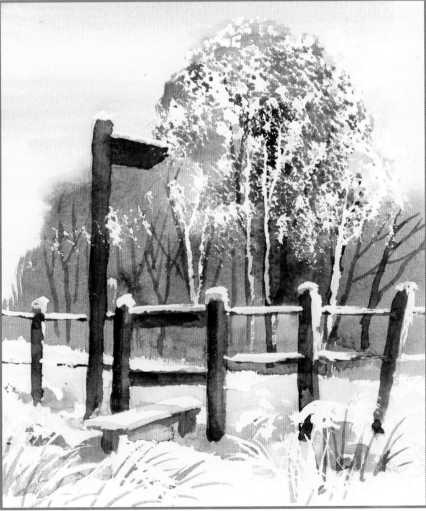

The finished painting.

163 GRASS GROWING THROUGH SNOW

To help break up a large area of white foreground, grass can be painted in with the fan gogh brush or a half-rigger. Another tip is to use a px (clear acrylic resin) brush handle to scrape out some grasses whilst the paint is still wet. This technique was also used to scrape out the tree trunks on the left.

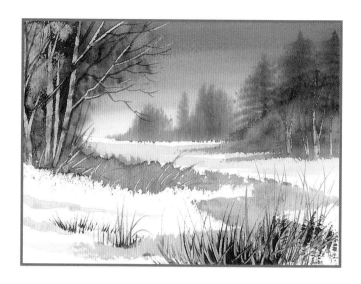

164 PAINTING SNOW SHADOWS

The colours for snow shadows can vary, but often use cobalt blue mixed with a little shadow colour. This gives me the desired effect, but depending on the lighting effects, these colours can change, so a variety of blues could be used. The important thing to remember is to avoid using grey.

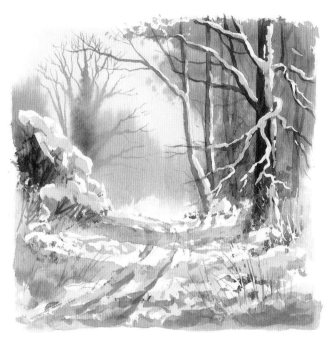

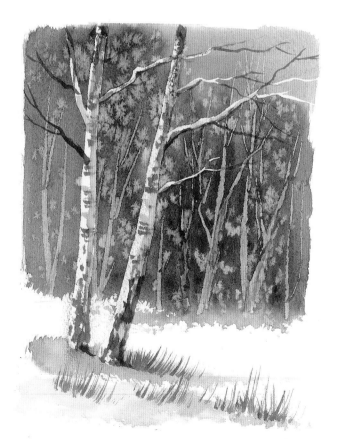

165 ADDING TEXTURE TO SNOW

An interesting effect can be achieved by sprinkling grains of salt on to wet paint. The salt absorbs the paint, leaving a starburst shape, which is ideal for suggesting snowflakes and frost. To get the best results from this technique, allow the paint to dry completely and in its own time (do not use a hairdryer), then dust off the salt particles.

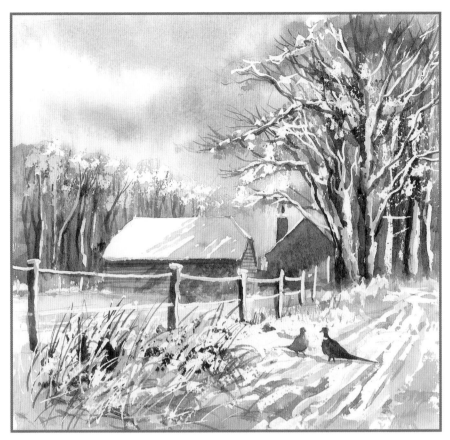

166 MASKING FLUID SNOW ON TREES

Masking fluid can be used to great effect when painting snow. Here I applied the masking fluid with a sponge for the treetops, and with a small brush for the snow that had settled on the branches and trunks. I used a ruling pen to apply the masking fluid to the fence and the grasses in the foreground. Some of the ruts and texture in the foreground were painted with masking fluid. After removing the masking fluid, a light wash of cobalt blue was applied to create some shadows, the rest was then left as white paper.

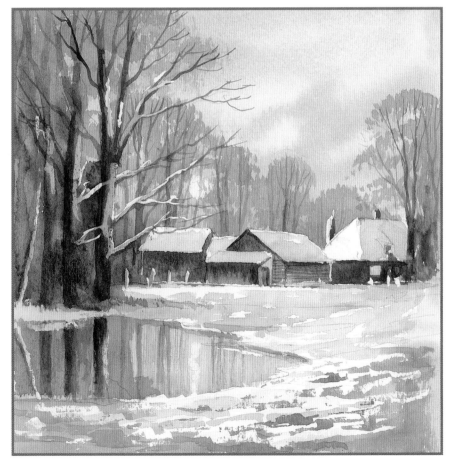

167 WARMING UP A SNOW SCENE

A snow scene does not necessarily have to be cold, frosty and unpleasant. If you paint a scene at sunset, this gives you the opportunity to introduce a whole variety of warm colours. Here I applied masking fluid in the same way as in the other examples, but I added the colours of the sunset reflected in the snow.

Pearse Street Branch
Brainse Sráid Piarsach
Tel: 6744888

Figures & animals

Simply adding a living creature to a painting can enhance it a great deal as it begins to tell a story rather than just being a pleasant view.

168 BOATMEN

This is a simple painting of two boats, but adding the figures makes it a different type of painting. The two boatmen suggest there is a conversation going on. It is a good tip to leave something to the imagination of the viewer.

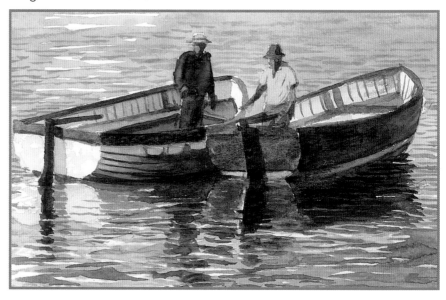

169 A MAN AND A DOG

This painting would be very simple and almost uninteresting without the man and his dog, but making them the focal point has created something a lot more substantial.

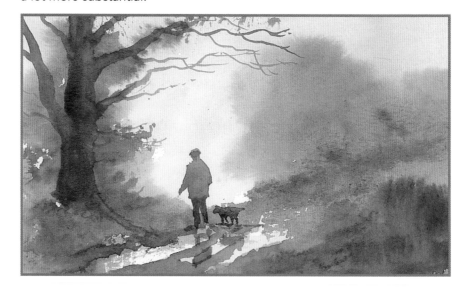

170 **WINTER WALK**

Placing the dog walker in the lane not only adds interest but also acts as a break, allowing the viewer to pause for a moment instead of being drawn deep into the distance.

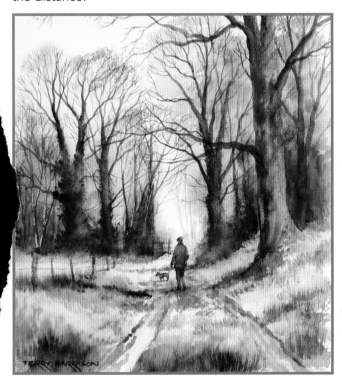

171 **BIRDS**

What makes a sunset painting interesting is usually not the actual sunset, but the scene it affects, for example the sun setting over an estuary, the silhouette of a group of trees or the outline of a windmill. If we have a sunset on its own with no landscape and we add a flock of birds, it becomes a painting in its own right.

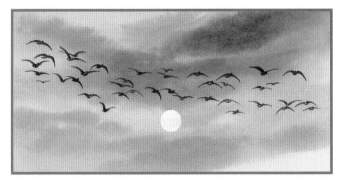

172 **COTTAGE WITH CHICKENS**

This charming painting of a thatched cottage is brought to life simply by adding a few chickens and the farmer's daughter. Without these added elements, the painting would merely be a building study.

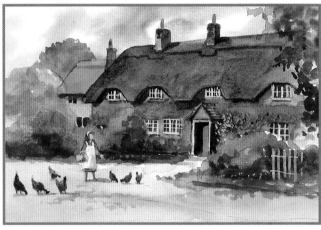

173 **PHEASANTS IN THE LANE**

This winter snow scene has plenty of interest such as the rustic barn and a snow-covered stile, with the lane drawing the viewer deep into the painting. The composition left an empty wide-open foreground. Placing the pair of pheasants into the middle of the lane adds that touch of colour and interest. Reference images for the pheasants can be found online.

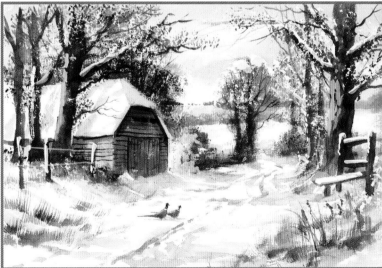

Index

B
Barn 27, 30, 127
Beach 8, 15, 22, 59, 101, 102–103, 107
Blossom 25, 79
Boat 22–24, 108–109, 126
Bridge 26, 115
Brushes 6, 8, 13–18, 20, 48
  Clear acrylic resin handle 13, 76, 84, 85, 112, 124
Brushstroke 34, 36, 85, 88, 96
Building 13, 26, 41, 74, 110, 112, 114, 116–117, 127

C
'Cauliflower' 20, 40, 62–64
Cliff 20, 101, 106–107
Cling film 21, 61, 106
Cloud 40, 42, 62–63, 67–70, 92, 107
Colour shaper 21, 51, 122
Colours 28–29, 30–33
  Basic palette 28, 30
  Ready-made greens 28, 32, 78
Composition 23, 26–27, 127
Cottage 25, 118, 127

D
Drawing 8, 20, 53, 108, 110

E
Effect 8, 13, 20–21, 36, 40–44, 52–53, 55, 58, 62–63, 74, 79, 81, 84, 93, 96, 104, 111, 117, 124

F
Field 16, 52, 74, 120
Flower 13, 28, 51, 86–91, 117–118
Focal point 25, 27, 126
Foliage 14, 55, 59–60, 79, 88, 102, 105, 113

G
Grasses 13, 17, 20, 36, 49, 51, 84–85, 87–88, 122–125

H
Hard lines 43, 62, 63
Hedge(row) 16, 52, 74
Highlight 68, 92
Hill 59, 72
Horizon 13, 59, 71, 99

K
Kitchen paper 8, 18, 20, 36, 44, 47, 53–57, 68, 70, 92, 100, 122

L
Landscape 11, 58, 66, 76, 120, 127

M
Magic watercolour eraser 21, 55–56
Masking fluid 8, 10, 20–21, 48–53, 79, 85–88, 92, 95–96, 98, 100–103, 107, 116–117, 121–123, 125
Mountain 20, 92–93

P
Paints 6, 18–19, 28–29
Palette 20, 29, 34–35, 38–39, 41
Paper 8, 10–12, 20, 22, 40, 44, 48, 56, 64–65, 79–81, 85, 104, 106
  Cockling 11, 65
  Tinted 10, 12
Paper mask 16, 52, 54, 56, 59
Perspective 67, 72
  Aerial 72–73
Photographs 8, 22, 24, 26–27
Plastic card 8, 20, 31, 80–81, 83, 93, 104, 107

R
Reference 22, 24, 26–27, 98, 127
Reflection 13, 46, 72, 97–98, 101, 107, 116
Resist 20, 59
  Candle wax 21, 59, 116
Ripples 13, 94, 96, 103
River 18, 24, 36, 94–95
Rock 8, 20, 31, 52, 58, 93–95, 98, 101, 104–105
Roof 41, 90, 110–111, 116
Ruling pen 20, 49, 85, 87, 125

S
Salt 21, 58, 124
Sea 52, 94, 99, 101, 107
Seascape 11, 31
Shadow 12, 28, 41, 54, 67, 69–70, 86, 90, 93, 103, 105, 110, 113–115, 117–119, 122–124
Sky/skies 12–13, 16, 24, 40, 42, 46–47, 53, 59, 66–72, 76, 87, 92, 99, 101, 107
Snow 12, 30, 49, 53, 92, 122–125, 127
Sponge 21, 52, 54–55, 57, 79, 100, 125
Spray 52, 98, 100
Sun 27, 56–57, 70, 93, 96, 117, 121, 127
Sunset 10, 12, 46, 70–71, 125, 127

T
Techniques
  Drop(ping) in 27, 40–41, 61–63, 67–69, 76, 86, 88, 93, 110–111, 113, 118–119, 122
  Dry brush 11, 44, 81–82, 106
  Glaze/glazing 46–47
  Lift(ing) out 20–21, 47, 54–56, 68, 70, 92, 96, 100
  Scrape/scraping out 13, 31, 76, 80, 83–85, 93, 97, 104, 107, 112–113, 115, 124
  Spattering 8, 50, 59, 102
  Stipple/stippling 13–17, 54, 78–79, 83, 88, 102, 104–105, 112–113
  Wash(es) 10, 11, 13, 18–19, 36, 38–42, 44, 46, 49–50, 58–59, 62, 65–66, 68, 72, 81, 85, 88, 92, 96–97, 99, 102–103, 113, 116–117, 119, 125
  Wet into wet 8, 40–43, 46, 53, 61–64, 66, 69–71, 76, 83, 86–87, 90, 93, 97, 101, 107, 118, 122
  Wet on dry 13, 43, 78
Texture 11, 13–15, 20–21, 31, 44, 52, 54, 58, 61, 80–81, 83, 85, 88, 104–107, 110, 112–114, 116–117, 124–125
Texture paste 21, 60, 118
Tone 20, 46, 73–74, 78, 89, 95
Tree 13–14, 16, 20, 25, 43–44, 53–55, 57, 71, 73, 76–83, 97–98, 116, 122–125, 127

W
Wall 13, 112–115
Watercolour ground 21, 60, 118
Waterfall 94–95
Wave 8, 98
Winter 10, 12, 78, 122–125, 127
Wood 10, 18, 24, 46, 57, 89, 115, 117, 123

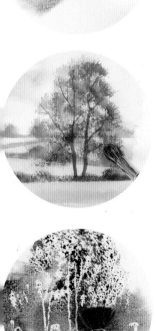

Ianna Poibli Chathair Bhaile Átha
Public Libraries